MW01127674

3 LEVELS of INFLUENCE

THE EXTRAORDINARY LIFE CHANGING POWER OF MENTORSHIP

3 LEVELS of INFLUENCE

THE EXTRAORDINARY LIFE CHANGING
POWER OF MENTORSHIP

By

Les Thomas Sr.

3 Levels of Influence
By Les Thomas Sr.

Copyright © 2022 Les Thomas

Cover Design: Scott Soliz, www.zealdesino.com

Publishing Coach: Randy Allsbury

Content Editor: Derrick Sier

Line Editor: Darnell Blake

Edited by Lori Haroldson

ISBN 13: 979-8842068753

All rights reserved. No part of this book may be re- produced or transmitted in any form or by any means, electronic or mechanical, including photocopying and recording, or by an information storage and retrieval system, without permission in writing from the author.

Table of Contents

Dedication

To Mary Elizabeth Rhoda Thomas – The most beautiful human being I've ever met, both inside and out. I've said many times that when people see me, they also see you. A sailboat has the potential to sail the seven seas, but without the wind, it can achieve nothing. You have been the constant wind and the driving force in my life that has allowed me to dream without hesitation. Thank you for always supporting me, even when my dreams are wild and crazy. You ask me the hard questions, and I could never accomplish anything great in this life without your strength and wisdom. Without your support I would not be who I am today. When I win, you win; we win.

To my babies, Lesso and Leilah Boo. Both of you have made me the proudest father on the planet. When you both were born, I was a kid. Thank you for having patience and grace with your old man through the growing pains over the years. As your parents, Mom and I have been a constant voice in your life. I pray that this book continues to be a voice in your life, even long after I'm gone. The principles in this book helped to lay the foundation of the father I would become. A man without many examples became an example. I pray that I have exemplified striving to be the best you can be, and I pray this book encourages you to be the best that you can be.

To my mother, Linda "Chilling in Heaven" Thomas. Not a single word I'm about to say can express my gratitude and thankfulness for you. You were my first best friend. Your belief in me from childhood was the fuel that propelled me to higher heights. Can you believe I'm an author? Wow! This is because of you! When the world wrote me off, you continued to see the best in me. We did everything together. We struggled together, and we celebrated together. I have no doubt that you are still celebrating with me. When I win, you win.

To my father and brothers. I wouldn't ask God for anyone else to be my father and brothers. You all support me, listen to me complain, give me sound words and advice. I'm grateful for our time together. Thank you for giving me space to be me. I've got a little of that Wilson blood in me so I can be a tough cookie at times. Love all of you to the moon and back.

To Mr. Green, my first mentor. Thank you for spending time with me, pouring into me, and for providing a safe place for this scrawny little boy to crash at your place often.

To Youth for Christ, my first training ground for mentoring. When I started working for YFC, I had been mentored but never understood the importance of being a mentor. Seventy-five percent of my knowledge of understanding the third level, written in this book, came from my years in YFC. Thank you Matt Hankinson and Marcus "Kadence" Jackson for bringing me on to serve with you.

Foreword

The struggle to find purpose is so real. The world we live in is filled with potential. Sadly, it also filled with wasted potential. I am just like everyone else when it comes to my search for purpose and discovering my God-given assignment. It has not been a simple journey, but the lack of ease has ultimately been rewarding. I can truly say that I am a person put on this earth to serve others.

There are multiple social issues that concern me. Issues such as poverty, crime, divorce rates, single parent homes, and youth living in group homes and foster care weigh heavy on my heart and mind. Many people see these social issues as a problem for someone else to solve. However, only a few people see these issues and believe that they are the solution. They believe God has given them the assignment to provide solutions to these problems. I have intentionally decided to be among the few and want desperately to be with others who have made the same daily sacrifice to serve others and to be a solution.

In 1996, I became a police officer, and I truly believe God blessed me with this opportunity to not only answer my personal prayers, but to satisfy my burning desire to serve my community. Being a native of Oklahoma City, it was only fitting that I serve in the place I had called home for my entire life. It wasn't long before my experiences as a patrolman revealed a deeper understanding of what it meant to serve others. There was more to be done to address incredibly pressing needs of the community. The negative changes in our society like street gangs, guns, and drugs were not only plaguing our adults in the community, but it was also taking a major toll on our young people. This birthed a deep conviction in me and inspired my passion to serve youth in at-risk communities in a more personal manner. I realized that police work is what I did, and it did not completely tell the full story of who I was.

Over the years, I've served the community in multiple ways, including establishing the Oklahoma City Police Department's first Gang Prevention and Youth Outreach Unit. This Unit is called F.A.C.T, which stands for Family Awareness and Community Teamwork. The unit focuses on mentorship, building character, and empowering at-risk youth which ultimately reduced juvenile delinquency and involvement with the criminal justice system. These full-time police unit hosts multiple programs including "Man Up", which is a program teaching teenage boys the primary principles of manhood. It was this experience, alongside my positive track record with inner city youth, which earned me the title of "Master Mentor."

As a "Master Mentor" I search for ways to use experiences God has blessed me with to pay it forward by providing wisdom and mentorship to someone in need. I have found a small group of committed community members who have this same desire. That's why, to this very day, I continually organize and implement opportunities for at-risk youth to connect with positive, caring adults who will help them realize their true authentic God-given potential. One of those positive and caring adults, who always answers the call and goes above and beyond, is actually the reason you and I are reading this book. Les Thomas, Sr. is a good friend, brother, and indigenous leader.

Ten years ago, I called on Les to help me with a community event that would be filled with hundreds of kids who were from difficult living situations. These types of events often send the casual volunteer home early. But not Les! People work in these types of spaces with me and other police officers for a couple of reasons. They volunteer for the reward, or they volunteer for the responsibility. If they are only working for the reward, you quickly realize the motivation is all about self-gain. If they are working for the responsibility, the motivation is all about others. Les worked with me because he truly cares about others, and he feels responsible for his community.

I have had over ten years of experience serving the community with Les, and I can honestly say that he is one of the most genuine and caring mentors I've come into contact with. He is the perfect person to write this book. I believe we can all be inspired to be the best version of ourselves with great mentorship and leadership. That's why I believe you should take the time to invest in yourself and read this life-changing book. I know Les has poured his heart and soul into this book, and now you have an opportunity to experience his heart and passion for mentorship the same way that I have for so many years. Every single time you are blessed to have time with Les you are left knowing God wanted your day to improve because Les takes your spirit to another level. Get ready to learn, grow, and be inspired from someone I know truly desires for you to succeed.

—**Wayland Cubit**, *Speaker/Master Mentor/Trainer*

Chapter 1

A TOUGH BEGINNING

It was a Friday.

It started as an ordinary day but ended as a night that would change my life forever.

When I was a boy, football games were what I lived for. Friday night football was the epicenter of everything cool. I absolutely loved going to the games! As a seven-year-old the energy in the air, the smells, and the sound of the band made Friday nights electrifying for me.

In my family, band was a way of life. I came from a long line of musicians. My brothers and I used to get pots, pans, and various buckets, and use spoons and forks as drumsticks. Hours would go by, and our mother never said a word. She believed in allowing us to use the gifts and talents that God gave us, even if it destroyed the very thing we needed to eat with. Nothing was off limits when it came to making music. With music being our first love, we never went to football games just to watch football. I couldn't tell you one person on the football team, but I could name many band members.

Normally, my mother let me roam at the games if I stayed with my friends. Because my mother was the type of woman that took care of many neighborhood kids, our family had a connection with numerous people. I've literally heard over a hundred kids call my mother "Momma Thomas." But on this night, she didn't feel good about letting me run around; but, after me pleading for what seemed like forever, she finally gave me her blessing. While tossing a football around in the west end zone with two friends, we suddenly noticed hundreds of people chaotically running and screaming. It was as if they were running for their lives. Then I heard it.

"Pow! Pow! Pow!"

Shots were being fired.

There originally were three of us, but only two of us ran. Wondering why our other friend wasn't with us, we stopped running and turned around. I saw him lying on the ground, screaming. His screams were drowning out the sounds of gunfire. Tears ran down my face. Fear seamed to choke me, and I stood there staring like a deer in headlights. My mind told me to run, but my body wasn't cooperating.

How could this be? We were just innocent kids having the time of our lives. It was like the world stopped. Suddenly, I could hear a sound in the distance.

"Les! Les! Les!"

It got louder and louder. I could hear my mother yelling my name through all the noise. Mind you, I was by the west endzone, and my mother was with the band by the east endzone. I came to and not only did I notice the chaos erupting around me, but I also realized the chaos going on within myself. This event brought chaos into my heart and mind, and it would take years for me to overcome the trauma it caused. Up until this moment, I thought my parents getting a divorce years prior was as bad as life could get. I could never have imagined this. This would send me down a path of accepting and embracing a life that should not exist for a child. Unfortunately, the chaotic noise that was created in my young heart that day didn't stop at the age of seven. I would hear this sound daily as if it were my own heartbeat. Any loud noise made me freeze up or duck down.

In was 1988, I was ten and in the fifth grade. Gangs were growing. I discovered that there was finally something I could belong to that accepted me for me. Something that, in a strange way, brought me comfort and helped to silence the noise in my heart. Not because it was a good thing, but because I was surrounded by people that were used to the chaos. Their lack of fear rubbed off on me, and I started a life that wasn't suitable for someone my age. I wouldn't say that I was a gang member. I was more of a wannabe. Being a wannabe meant you were affiliated with a gang and pretty much did everything that a gang member did, but you weren't "officially" in the gang. Influence is one of the most powerful resources in our lives. I was always considered a leader among my peers, but with this, I completely gave into peer pressure and became a product of my environment.

During this time, my mother had me heavily involved in church. We went to church at least three or four times a week. I played the drums and participated in everything the church had available for my age group. Church was a safe place for me. Almost like a refuge. It was the only place I could relax and not worry about danger. Attending church was a way of life, and godly principles were instilled in me from birth. My mother was completely committed to God, and she loved God deeply. She prayed every single night, sometimes for hours. She did the best she could with me, but the noise in my head was too loud. My heart and emotions were filled with a sound that just wouldn't go away. I needed someone to tell me that it was going to be alright; but with no strong male voice to do that or to help guide me, the noise from the gunshots became my guide.

Because of the noise in my head and the need I felt to laugh, I became a class clown in the fifth grade. I found out that I could really make people laugh. I was a wannabe stand-up comedian and a wannabe gang member which was a true recipe for trouble in all kinds of ways. When I think about it, all I wanted was attention. The absence of a father in my life led me down a path in which I has no idea which way I should go. My mother was a phenomenal caretaker, but the absence of my father was hard to overcome. My father was around occasionally. He gave my mother child support, and I stayed with him from time to time; but there is nothing like having a father consistently and intentionally in your life.

At this time of my life, I found myself with my mother sitting in our living room, staring at a pink piece of paper from Green Pastures Fifth Grade School. The paper was notifying us that I failed. The embarrassment was real. I remember watching my mother cry. She called me over to her, and through her tears she told me everything would be all right. There was nothing like a warm embrace from my mother telling me that everything would be all right. When my mother said that I absolutely believed it. My mother was a God-fearing woman. But if you messed with her boys, you had better look out. That five-foot, three-inch woman would transform into Wonder Woman.

The next day, we went to the Oklahoma City Public School Administration Office, and we were told that they would pass me if I went to summer school and did well. Because my older brother was heading to Millwood for summer school, my mother sent me with him. We had very limited resources, but somehow, she came up with the money. That was my mother for you. She would give her boys anything and would do anything short of immoral to provide for us. Oftentimes, in the mornings before school, I would steal change out of my brother's car or my mother's purse so I could buy Starbursts from the vending machine. My favorite thing to do was unwrap all the Starbursts and form them into one big ball. Imagine trying to eat a piece of candy bigger than your mouth. That was the way I liked it!

I did well both semesters of summer school. I walked out with all A's and a nice recommendation letter from my teacher. Feeling fully confident with the results, my mother and I took my report card and recommendation letter up to OKCPSA so I could go on to the sixth grade. The superintendent refused to see us, and they told us that because Millwood District was not an Oklahoma City Public School that my report card would not be accepted. All that hard work, and not to mention my mother coming up with money that I know she didn't have, and still back to fifth grade I went.

After repeating the fifth grade, I proceeded to go to middle school. This is when my first mentor, Mr. Green, entered my life. I knew him prior to sixth grade, but this is when we started spending time together. He was tall, dark-skinned, and had a voice that penetrated to the core of your soul. Mr. Green was known in the neighborhood for being a stand-up guy. Because we didn't have many men in our neighborhood, people looked to him for guidance and safety. He was like the official neighborhood dad.

Mr. Green spent an abundance of time with me, and it meant the world to me. I never knew why he would want to hang out with a skinny boy that had a speech impediment and nothing to offer. I'm not sure he knew exactly why either. Since he knew we didn't have much money, he would hire me to do various jobs around the neighborhood. Every weekend Mr. Green would pull his 1955 Buick out and clean it from top to bottom. I sat there and watched in admiration and confusion. It looked clean to me, but he cleaned it as if he just drove down a dirt road. It was so clean I could see my reflection in the chrome.

I would ask, "Mr. Green why are you always cleaning your car?"

He would say, "Boo, you take care of the things you love."

He cared for his grass in the same way. I often wondered if his grass were real because I never recall it needing cut. He had to be cutting his grass twice a week. It was thick, green, and had the straightest lines I had ever seen. He paid me to cut other yards, but one day I asked Mr. Green if I could cut his yard. He initially said no, but who could turn down this big-eared boy looking disappointed. He reluctantly said yes, and I soon found out why. He wanted to cut his grass a certain way with no mistakes. I remember cutting and thinking that I was doing a great job, but he kept correcting me. You would have thought CNN was coming to do a show on his grass the way he was critiquing me. Seemed like nothing I did was right. I eventually got frustrated because I thought it was perfect and wanted to quit, but he wouldn't let me. Instead, he chose to fuss with me and teach me. I remember him teaching me that I should always finish any job I started.

You see, he was teaching me how to pay attention to detail and challenging me to give my best. Taking my time and doing it right was better than going fast and not being satisfied with the results. Now, I never asked to cut his grass again, but in hindsight I learned so much from that moment. I loved being around Mr. Green. I loved it so much that I would sit in silence in his garage while he worked on a car or cleaned his already-super-clean garage. Now this was in 1990 when there were no handheld games, cell phones, or TVs in garages. Sitting there doing nothing was good for me. It was like I knew that he had something that I needed; and he knew I had something that he needed. We are wired to give ourselves away. We naturally want to lead and help others. But what could I possibly give a well-established, successful man? Mr. Green had no kids living with him, just he and his wife, Mrs. Ester. And at that time, I was giving Mr. Green something that his wife, kids, and job couldn't give. Purpose. Assignment. An opportunity to impart wisdom, teach, develop, and pour into someone that needed it desperately. I wasn't wise enough to understand why I needed him, but what I did know, is that I felt safe and valued in his presence. Mr. Green impacted my life like no other man had. There was finally a voice that could silence the noise.

In sixth grade, the school I attended was like a war-zone. We had several fights and brawls because of gang activity. Our school installed metal detectors because fights and brawls caused by gang activity were a current event. We would fight the teachers when they tried to give us swats. This is part of the reason corporal punishment was taken out of schools. Not because of teachers, but because students would fight back. I managed to escape the sixth grade without getting in too much trouble. But seventh grade was lurking around the corner. When I was in seventh grade, my friends and I got into a confrontation with some people. Confrontation was normal at this age in my neighborhood. But this confrontation was a little different, and we wanted to retaliate. The people we had a disagreement with went on a vacation, and we decided to break into their house. Initially we just wanted to eat their food and destroy a few things. But, as the night went on, it got cold, so we started a fire in the fireplace. Well, that gave us the dumb idea to start burning some of their belongings. Next thing you know, we're putting things in the fire faster than they could burn. You can guess what happened next. The fire extended out of the fireplace onto the carpet and onto the furniture. We ran out of the house, and by the time we got to the end of the street, you could see flames in the air. We burned the house to the ground.

I remember running home. My mother knew me very well, and she asked me what was going on. I didn't tell her at first. Since it was a Friday night, we jumped in the car to head to church. At church, I just couldn't stop crying. She again asked me what was wrong, and this time I couldn't hold back. I told her that my friends and I had burned a house down. You would have thought Jesus walked into the room. It's like all the blood in her body left for a few moments. I thought she was going to start beating me in the middle of church. Somehow, she maintained her composer. We left, but a fifteen-minute car ride felt like eternity. That was one the hardest conversations I ever had with my mom. Even through all the trouble I got into in the past, I knew that this moment would change my life.

It really didn't matter if I told my mom or not because the police were at our door the next day. I was busted. People say that snitches get stitches; but what if the snitch might kill me if I tried to give him stitches? That was the predicament I was in. I never addressed getting snitched on. Nonetheless, I ended up going before a judge over this incident, and I remember it like it was yesterday. Driving to the courthouse, I felt like everything was in slow motion. When we arrived at the courtroom it smelled like an old musty building and almost every seat was filled. You could feel the tension in the air. I was so scared and full of shame for putting my mother through this embarrassment.

The judge called my mother and me up to the stand. I couldn't move my legs. No matter how hard I tried, my body wouldn't cooperate. I felt paralyzed. My mother did one of those, "Boy you better bring yourself up here" gestures, and then I finally moved. The judge looked mad, as if it were her house we burned down. As I stood there with my mom looking at the ground with tears in my eyes, I remember feeling like I was about to get hit by a train. A silent train. I could hear myself breathing. The judge cleared her throat and began to speak with authority and passion while sentencing me. My mother suddenly grabbed my face. She put her face close to mine and looked me directly in the eyes. You could hear everyone gasp wondering what was going on. What happened next changed my life.

My mother interrupted the judge and said these words to me, "Les, this moment will not define you. You're not a bad kid. God has called you to do great things. Do not allow this judge or anyone else to make you think or believe that you are a bad person. You have been called by God to accomplish great things. I rebuke Satan! He cannot have you. I have known that you were called from the time you were in my womb. You will go on to do great things."

She released my face and stood back up facing the judge. The courtroom was completely silent. The judge had stopped talking and no one said anything for at least twenty seconds. In the end, the judge dismissed the case. I did have to do community service, but what impacted me the most was not the punishment. It was what my mother told me. It made me wonder if my mother ever read Johann Wolfgang's quote that said, "Look at a man the way he is, and he only becomes worse; but look at him as if he were what he could be, then he becomes what he should be."

I continued to the seventh grade at Rogers Middle School. Although my mom was a godly woman and very intentional, my home was still lacking something. I still wanted to get attention. I had no self-control and was full of anger. I soon got into a fight with a teacher and promptly found myself kicked out of school. That was so hard for my mom. You see, she had tried to transfer me to Millwood Middle School in fifth grade, but the school wouldn't allow me because I already had a record at that age. Now I was kicked out of school, and my mom didn't know what to do with me.

My Uncle Paul and Aunt Olivia Purvey lived within the Millwood school district. My mother knew the only way I could get into Millwood Middle School was if we used their address. Knowing that I was denied before, the only way I could use the address was if my mother gave up custody of me. This was hard for my mother to do, but she knew that in order for her son to survive, this had to be done. My mother loved me so much that she was willing to give up her parental rights so I could have a better life. My uncle and aunt then became my legal guardians. I am very thankful that they took me in. My mom cried and cried over this. I recall telling her, "Mom, I'm still going to live with you."

I didn't understand in the moment how hard it was for her to give up her parental rights. At the time, I couldn't see that her love for me and her desire for me to succeed was the only thing that mattered to her. She would do whatever it took. I didn't fully understand the sacrifice she made for me until I got older.

Through all of this, Mr. Green was still there for me. He loved me so much that he even asked my mother if she wanted him to help discipline me. That's love. Mr. Green was just a man in the neighborhood that happened to take a liking to me. For him to say that he would join my mom in bringing correction to me was a love like no other. I had nothing to offer Mr. Green. Yet, he loved me. Eventually the gang activity became too much, so Mr. Green moved away.

After all of this happened, my mother made sure I didn't have time for foolishness. School, band, church, and home were the only places I had time for. We started going to church even more. I'll never forget the time I met the new youth minister, Minister Gray.

Minister Gray was a cool, young, youth pastor who was really down to earth. My church was very legalistic. It was all about how perfect you looked on the outside. Our church was an older church filled with older men, so I couldn't relate to most of them. It was very hard to maneuver through all of the pressure that was put on members to reflect a perfect life at the church. For the most part, regular conversation about life didn't exist. We couldn't talk about temptation, anger, football, or any real-life situations without being judged. This was not the case with Minister Gray though. He was a breath of fresh air because he talked to us about everything, such as, football, girls, life, and music. His hair had waves for days, and he wore Dior's Fahrenheit cologne. He dressed nicely and listened to The Isley Brothers.

I was in high school at the time that Minister Gray started attending our church, and although I wasn't getting into too much trouble, I still had that rebellious side that needed guidance. By this time, I was into girls, and I needed much guidance. Minister Gray was my go-to for navigating the dating scene. I talked to him about every girl that I liked. His house was the spot to hang out at. My friends and I were always over at his house hanging out and he just experienced life with us. We didn't always have lesson after lesson with Minister Gray; it was more of an up-close look at how a man operated with his family. In my neighborhood, I could count on one hand how many fathers were involved, so that was something we weren't used to.

Another great mentor while I was in high school was our ROTC instructor Sergeant Dubose. He did not put up with any nonsense and demanded discipline. He quickly recognized the leadership skills I possessed, and he kept a close eye on me. I couldn't get away with anything. He called me out often. I can't tell you how many push-ups I had to do. He would tell me that he was hard on me because I had more to give. That didn't register in my mind for years because I was too busy thinking about how I didn't have a job, my family was poor, I owned nothing, and some of the possessions I did have were stolen. What could he possibly mean that I had more to give? He recognized that I had a habit of doing just enough just to get by.

I remember one day a student and I almost got into a fight. He said, "So you think you're tough guys, aye?" He told us to go outside, and he made us hold our arms out parallel to the ground. Then, he made us do small and big circles. I can hear his voice as I'm typing.

"Hold it, hold it."

I thought my arms were going to fall off. The main thing that sticks out to me about this moment is that he did it with us. The thing that confused me was that he was the one in charge. He did nothing wrong. And yet he was putting himself through pain with us. Talk about my respect level going through the roof. After that moment, I decided I would run through a brick wall for him, because it's one thing to help someone from a distance while they're in the valley, but it's another to walk through the valley with them. He never had any more problems from me.

Once again, I felt safe because a mentor took me in and allowed me in his life for my benefit. It's one of the most selfless things someone can do. I'm not sure if Mr. Green, Minister Gray, or Sgt. Dubose understood the impact they made on my life just by pulling me in and doing life with me. They were mentors to me, perhaps without even knowing that was what they were doing. I should not be where I am today. But because of God, my mother, and strong mentors in my life, it changed the trajectory of my life. I am truly a product of being mentored.

This book has been a labor of love. My hope and desire for you as you read it, is that you would gain as much out of it as possible. In each chapter you'll find multiple questions that invite you to process the chapter specific concept. At the end of each chapter, you'll find a section that I've called: *THINK ABOUT IT.* My challenge for you is to not only read, but to engage. I love what Benjamin Franklin said, *"I would advise you to read with a pen in your hand… for this is the best method of imprinting your memory."*

THINK ABOUT IT.

Who can you identify in your life that has mentored you? Even if he or she never official labeled themselves as a mentor, what did they do that impacted you the most? Explain.

_____

_____

_____

_____

_____

_____

_____

_____

_____

_____

_____

_____

_____

_____

Chapter 2

THREE LEVELS
OF INFLUENCE

"Having a mentor is a brain to pick, an ear to listen, and a push in the right direction."

--John Cosby

"Show me your friends and I'll show you your future."

--Jim Rohn

In this chapter, we will talk about the three levels of influence. But before we talk about the three levels, let's talk about influence itself. What is influence? Influence is the capacity to influence the character, development, or behavior of someone. We use influence in our everyday life. Sometimes it's intentional and sometimes it just happens.

Influence in the wrong hands can start wars, destroy churches and organizations, bring confusion, destroy families, start organized crime, cause division, and corrupt good people. However, influence in the right hands can end wars, impact generations, bring peace, encourage, inspire, create champions, build future leaders, unify, or set you on a pathway to greatness. Clint Eastwood said, "It takes tremendous discipline to control the influence, the power you have over other people's lives."

As a kid, my teachers always told my mother that I carried strong influence. On bad days I would use my influence the wrong way, and on good days I used my influence the right way. If you think about it, in your life, the way you usually use your influence is based on how you're feeling about a person, place, or thing. That's why it's important to be mentally healthy. When you're in a position of influence, you can't afford to be unstable.

One day, I remember my teacher making me upset. We had some words, and my pride went into overdrive. Peer pressure can make you do some crazy things. I told the class, "We're not doing any work today." My teacher responded aggressively and told me to shut up. What did I do? I stood up out of my seat, stuck my chest out, balled up my fists, and doubled down and said, "We are not doing any work today and you can't make us. Try me." Unfortunately, I had so much influence that the entire class sat there with me and did not work. That day I decided to use my influence in a negative way. Other days, I used my influence in positive ways. If I liked the teacher I would say, "Hey, get quiet. Let's listen and do what we're supposed to do." The class would listen to me and follow my example.

My question to you is, how are you using your influence? Better yet, what influences you? Are you influenced by facts? Are you influenced by fiction? Your inner circle? Are you influenced by TV or the news? What about social media? Are you influenced by truth? Everything that you attach yourself to influences you.

Now let's look at the three levels of influence. Let's imagine as if you're looking up in the sky and you see a plane in the air. That plane is level one. That plane is taking you to your destination. Let's process how you got on the plane

When you arrived at the airport, you looked for signs telling you where to go. Once inside, you found your airline and went to the check-in line. After checking in, you proceeded to the security checkpoint where your pathway is roped off, so you know where to go. After going through security, you look for directions to get to the correct terminal. These directions led you to the correct terminal to board your plane and head to your destination.

Now imagine checking into an airport with no assistance, no help, no signs, or directions. How would you know which airline to check-in with? How would you know the way to security checkpoint? After security, which terminal would you go to? It would simply be chaos. Without directions, you wouldn't know where to go.

Because there were directions, you knew where to go, and now you're headed to your destination. That is essential. That's what a mentor does for your life; a mentor gives you directions that best fit your life. They help you move toward the purpose for your life. A mentor doesn't tell you your destination. They help you get to your destination. They give you guidance and tell you things that challenge you. They may not always tell you what you want to hear, but it's for your own good so you do not miss your flight. Even in a delay, instructions can be given so you can prepare for the next flight.

Now, let's talk about the second level. These are your friends, your family, your co-workers, your neighbors. The people at this level help shape you, and help you digest what you've learned throughout your life. These are the people that you talk with, argue with, and discuss the things you've learned. This level is very important because it helps you discover your "why." I believe that your "why" is more important than your "how" and "when." Why do you believe what you believe? If your "why" is fragile or not pure, you can possibly find yourself operating from the wrong motive.

Your mentor gave you directions or helped you find your purpose. But how did you process or deal with the directions that were given to you? When you talk to people at this level, they challenge your thinking. In return, you need to challenge their thinking. This is called the iron sharpening level. I believe this level is just as important as the other levels. We will dive deeper into this level later.

Now let's talk about the third level. This is the level where you are pouring into others. This doesn't mean that people are beneath you. It is now your challenge to take everything you learned in levels one and two and pour it into the next person.

Michelle Obama said, "We should always have three friends in our lives. One who walks ahead who we look up to and follow; one who walks beside us, who is with us every step of our journey; and the one who we reach back for and bring along after we've cleared the way."

You now have an abundance of information, and it's your duty to help someone else. A mentor helped you in level one, your friends helped you in level two, and it is now your responsibility to pour into the next level. This produces the chain effect. It's the gift that keeps on giving. It has been proven that you learn more when you teach than when you receive. Since you received from a mentor, it's only right that you pay it forward and have a mentee.

This mentee is a future leader that has a destination and a destiny; but they need guidance and instruction that will help them along the way. Your job isn't to tell them their destiny. Your job is to give direction to them to help them reach their destiny.

Many people struggle with purpose and destiny. If you apply these three levels to your life, they will help you discover your destiny and your calling. They will help balance you and help you to become a better person. Proper understanding and use of influence is the key to maximize the potential in your life. It will bring a satisfaction like no other, and it will help you reach a purpose-fulfilled life.

THINK ABOUT IT.

Chapter 3

WHY DO LIFE ALONE?

Too much idle time can be a bad thing. When faced with great difficulties, it can be easy to recluse ourselves. When this happens, shame, self-pity, anxiety, and depression increase; and our sense of direction is minimized. Life is too valuable to do it alone.

A boxer can't become great without a team, and more specifically, a coach. When the fighter is training, it's rare that they are alone. There something about having someone with you cheering you on. They may not be doing the physical activities with you, but their presence gives you an extra boost. Your coach matters. It's not your job to come up with the strategy and game plan. Imagine how much energy would be taken away from you if you had to do everything yourself. It would hinder your training. Your coach is with you every step of the way. Their voice and you become one. When you step into the ring, there may be thousands of people there yelling, but there's only one voice that you are in tune with. While the fight is going on, you are listening to your coach. The coach is constantly making adjustments so you can win the fight. When the round ends and you go to your corner, one person patches up injuries while another person massages. Still, another gives water, and another applies petroleum jelly to the face. While all of this is going on, a coach is talking to you, guiding you to the next move, and making adjustments. Sometimes when you're in the fight of life, it's hard to process everything yourself. Like a boxer, one wrong move and you may find yourself on the ground.

That's what a mentor is in your life. They help you make adjustments. Whenever you're hit, they tell you how to block, how to counterpunch, or how to overcome. You're more likely to be knocked out fighting on your own, not making changes and corrections, than if you're listening to someone in your corner telling you how to make adjustments in the fight. Your coach is looking at the fight from a different angle so he can see things that you can't. While you're in the fight, your view is limited. While you're protecting your finances, your marriage may be hit; or while you're protecting your marriage, your health may be hit. A boxer can't protect his entire upper body with just two arms. He must move and do his best to protect himself from the onslaught of punches. This is hard to do when your eyes are closed or swollen from the blows of life. The voice becomes your guidance and your hope.

You can't fight life by yourself. You have a greater chance at winning the fight with someone in your corner. Having someone with you increases your confidence.

A military without a general can win a battle, but not

a war. There are more than one million citizens serving in the military. Imagine them fighting for our country with no guidance. Guidance produces integrity, discipline, and direction. It teaches you how to think under pressure and how to fulfill your duty.

I served for twenty years in the United States Air Force, and we were each assigned a mentor. Once a week in the military, we would gather with our supervisor. Our supervisor would then gather with their supervisor, and on and on all the way up to the commander of the base. That commander would then send out guidance to each unit giving them instructions on their duties. But then it was our job to carry out that duty.

The commander acted as a mentor – like our first level. Then he would speak to the leaders in each unit – our second level. Those leaders would then pass it down to everyone else in that unit – our third level. So, in a sense, we were being mentored from afar from our commander. Without guidance, we wouldn't know what to carry out. We wouldn't know what goal or task was at hand if it were not passed down to us. There is strength in numbers.

Helen Keller said, "Alone we can do a little; together we can do so much."

Denzel Washington also said, "Show me a successful individual and I'll show you someone who had real positive influences in his or her life. I don't care what you do for a living—if you do it well, I'm sure there was someone cheering you on or showing the way. A mentor."

A mentor gives you a much better chance at maximizing your abilities.

No one is self-made. Think about when you watch the Oscars, the Grammys, VMAs, or any other awards show. When the award is given out, the winner may say a few things in the beginning or give honor to God. The thing that happens next is they thank everyone that played a role in them attaining that goal and winning that award. Some thank so many that they are interrupted by music because their time is up. They say thank you because that guidance and teamwork helped them get to the place where they are now being honored for their accomplishment. I truly believe that it is impossible to maximize your potential without help. When you do make it to the top of your personal mountain, always show gratefulness to those that helped you.

The first two years of my marriage, I did life alone, and it wasn't enjoyable. I was a horrible husband. I was a horrible father. At that time, I asked myself often, what is a husband? What is a father? And because I didn't have a mentor in my life at the time to help guide me, my marriage suffered for two years. I had no accountability and no guidance. I broke remote controls, plates, cups, furniture, and doors. My wife and I would fight, and she would continually tell me that I needed to get help. The more she would tell me I needed to get help, the more I would rebel. This only caused us both to suffer.

Pride not only kills you, but it can kill your relationships. It wasn't until I got a mentor two or three years into my marriage that it really turned around. I was able to be brutally honest about the things I was doing in our home. And as uncomfortable as it was, I felt so liberated after opening up. This mentor helped guide me through my anger and my anxiety. They helped me when I didn't know what to do or how to respond to my wife and kids. If it were not for a mentor, I am sure that my marriage would have failed.

Not only did I get a mentor, but my wife got a mentor as well. We quickly found out that we could not do life alone, and we could not do our marriage alone. We not only surrounded ourselves with individual mentors, but we also had marriage mentors that we were able to be brutally honest with. They helped us realize that we could not walk our marriage alone.

Because of mentors, I'm a much better man, husband, father, brother, and friend. Search your perimeters. Search your life and ask yourself what areas you are trying to navigate alone.

I also challenge you to seek out a mentor. Mentors won't always come to you. In fact, most of the time, they usually don't come to you. You have to seek out a mentor. The people that you are around may not notice that you are suffering in certain areas because they only know what you tell them about your life. You know what areas you're suffering in alone, and I challenge you to seek out a mentor to help you in that area. We simply can't do life alone. Everyone needs someone. No one is self-made. It is impossible to attain greatness without having guidance, direction, and people in your corner.

We've all heard the quote that teamwork makes the dream work. A basketball team without a coach can win the game but not a championship. A coach gives you the X's and O's of the game. There are five people on the court at the same time with the goal of winning. Those five people without direction can win a few games, but the team that's coached well can win the championship. Michael Jordan isn't Michael Jordan without Phil Jackson. Kobe Bryant isn't Kobe Bryant without Phil Jackson. Magic Johnson isn't Magic Johnson without Pat Riley. All of these guys have tremendous skill and the ability to be great; but without a coach, it would be impossible for them to maximize their potential. If they had an attitude of thinking they could do it alone, they would not have been champions. Don't just win games. Bring home the gold!

THINK ABOUT IT.

Chapter 4

WHO ARE YOUR MENTORS?

I don't know what your family reunions, holidays, or summer weekends looked like, but when I was younger, it was always a good time when the grill was lit. Those days are imprinted on my mind like the grill lines on an all-beef hotdog. All the men sat around the grill and argued about sports and politics. The ladies gathered in small groups in the kitchen making side dishes. The elders would be soaking up the shade under a tree, or they would be in the house talking about whatever they used to do back in the day. The kids were scattered all over and around the house, but you could always find me standing next to the grill. Maybe it was my desire to get a cut of the grown-up meat. Maybe it was the fire, smoke, and smell of charcoal which grabbed my attention. Maybe it was the adult conversation that intrigued me; but whatever it was, I've always been drawn toward the grill.

I can remember one of the first times I grilled on my own and at my own place. My Grandma Etta gave me some huge T-bone steaks to grill. I had so much pressure on me because I had to save one steak for her. Surprisingly, the steaks turned out amazing! The smile on my grandmother's face told me everything. Before I left her house, she gave me some more steaks to grill in the future. I felt like a champ because she was happy, and I learned so much that day. But my biggest lesson didn't come while cooking. It came the next day while prepping to cook out again.

As I prepped, I removed the old ashes from the grill and placed them in a brown paper bag. I just knew they had cooled off because all I could see were grey ashes. Everything had burned up and there were no signs of heat. I went inside to get the meat ready, and, upon my return, I saw smoke. I was confused because I hadn't started the fire yet. The bag was completely on fire, and it was leaning up against our building. My heart was racing as if I was Usain Bolt on the last stretch of the 200m. With no time to run inside to grab water, I had nothing but my feet to put it out. I stomped the fire out like I was on Stomp the Yard; except my yelling wasn't a chant and had no kind of sequence. Just plain screaming. Not to long after that, barbecuing was banned in our apartments. This was a hard lesson about cooking out; but rest assured, it taught me to never underestimate the heat that coals maintain even days later. Even with all that being said, barbecuing is still my thing. Now, I consider myself to be a humble man; but because of my history with the grill, I lose ninety percent of my humility when it comes to putting meat on the fire. It's my spot. My place. It's where I can momentarily disconnect from the pressures of real life and focus in on my love for cooking.

What sets my barbecue apart from other's barbecue is the time, attention, and detail that I give to seasoning the meat. I clearly think about what I want my meat to taste like, and I grab all the ingredients that I need. I could just stick to the one major ingredient, and that is salt; but if I only used salt, I am doing a disservice to the meat. I'm not enhancing or maximizing the flavor and the potential that's in the meat. You see, all the good flavor is in the meat; but if it's not unified with the proper seasonings, the potential flavor will lie dormant. If I just use salt, it will taste okay. But the more ingredients I bring in, the better the meat will taste. I love to cook steak! It is one of my favorite meats to eat. I use salt, pepper, olive oil, Worcestershire sauce, soy sauce, and garlic salt. I also add in a little bit of Creole-Cajun seasoning, dried mustard powder, and... I can't reveal the rest. Like a grandmother, I don't tell everybody all my cooking secrets.

While I'm cooking out and sitting there, I get to unlock parts of my brain that are usually shut down because I have so much going on in life. Much needed "me time" takes place while I'm grilling. Sometimes I bring my phone and scroll through social media, but many times I leave my phone inside and just take in the outdoors. After seasoning the meat, I must then focus on keeping the temperature at a certain level. But grilling doesn't seem like work to me. I enjoy it so much that I don't mind the tedious work that it takes to satisfy my family and friends' taste buds. All of these things bring a juicy and delectable steak to my table.

Like having multiple seasonings to bring out the flavor in the steak, I believe that we need multiple mentors to bring out the potential that's already in us. Having a single mentor is a great start. With only a single mentor, however, you take a chance of becoming stagnant and complacent. You run into the possibility of areas of your life being untouched. It's rare that one person can cover all the areas of your life. Some mentors thrive in specific areas such as finances, family guidance, marriage guidance, professional career and so on. If you have only one mentor, that individual may come into a season in their life where they're not as available. Life happens to everyone. Just like you have certain areas that you're weak in, your mentor may have a similar weak area.

A lot of times when we consider a mentor, we think about just the business side. We think about how we just want to have a mentor that can help in the business world and in your professional career. Well, what about your personal life? What about making sure that you're well rounded? If you're succeeding in your professional career but failing at home, your life is out of balance. The inverse is true, too. If you're succeeding at home but failing in your professional career, your life is out of balance.

In other words, if you limit yourself to one mentor, you are intentionally putting a lid on your life where you can't go as high as your potential can take you. Having multiple mentors is like having your own advisory board. When I'm going through something in my life, sometimes I like to bounce it across multiple people and multiple mentors. That way I can get different perspectives. This helps me to develop my own perspective.

Mentorship is something that is very intentional. Just remember, it is possible to spread yourself thin with too many mentors. I believe a mentor and a mentee must be intentional and make time to talk and to build and to develop their relationship. Be mindful of having too many mentors.

If you have a desire to start a business, you might want to go to someone in that field and ask if they can mentor you. While that person may be an expert in that field, it doesn't necessarily mean they can help you in your personal life. They may not be able to help you with other challenges you're facing.

I've always had three to five mentors. I was in my mid-twenties when I first realized that I needed multiple mentors. During this time my mentor was a spiritual mentor. He mentored me, guided me spiritually, and helped me with my personal relationship with God. He taught me how to pray, how to fast, and everything that comes along with being a follower of Christ. With his guidance, I was able to determine my calling and do the work of the Lord.

When my calling was revealed to me, the church became my life. I would go to work from 6:30 a.m. until 5:00 p.m., then drive straight to the church. Many weekends were taken up by the church as well. I'd paint, cut grass, work on sheds, build whatever needed to be built, clean, and whatever else I could do to help the church. And I always served in some kind of capacity. Anything that needed to be done, I did it. I sometimes wouldn't get home until 9:30 or 10:00 at night. To add insult to injury, I was part of a Christian Rap group that had concerts literally every week. If I wasn't at church, I was on the road. Don't get me wrong. I reaped lots of fruit during this time of my life, and it introduced me to my first intentional strong mentor, Nick Smith. Sure, Mr. Green had been a mentor to me before Nick, but Nick is really the first mentor relationship that I intentionally sought to establish.

Nick was like a big brother to me. We're both country boys. We like to fish and hunt, and we did that on many occasions. We didn't always talk on specific topics, but I learned so much from having unstructured time just hanging with him. These were some of the most formidable years of my life. Because we were under the same leader and the rap group was his idea, we were constantly around each other. Those were some of the best days of my life! Nick had a way of correcting me, teaching me, and loving me like I had never been loved before. Since I admired him and looked up to him, submitting myself to his leadership as a mentor was easy for me. He was carrying something that I needed; so, I asked him to be my mentor. You see, up until this point, I was always one of the leaders in my pack. I was used to having no accountability, and my friends encouraged my wild living. Finally, someone, outside of my wife and mother, saw the potential in me. Up until I met him, only my mother spoke to that childlike faith in me to dream big. As I was becoming an adult, life tried to choke that part out of me. Finally, I had someone in my life that truly believed in me and helped me to crush the doubt of my potential.

We cannot be afraid to ask someone that we know we need in our lives to mentor us. Pride and ego cannot get in the way of destiny. I went from no identity, full of anger, with no direction to being developed into a leader. Nick's style of mentoring me wasn't at a table across from each other. He just did life with me. Every time we were together, we had in-depth conversation.

It was these conversations that helped me become the music artist I am today. God used him to pull out my gift of music. It laid dormant until he challenged me to write and work with him. And I'm still doing music seventeen years later! We talked about being a husband and a father. We talked about how to fish and how to hunt better. He was a multi-facetted mentor in my life. He helped me become an overall better man. My individual growth blossomed during this time, but my home was still lacking growth collectively.

I often tell people that the church became my mistress. I worked as if I could earn favor with God through doing work. My lack of being raised with my father made me think that the more I worked for Him, the more I would be accepted and loved.

My life was so out of balance because all the other areas of my life were suffering. People would look at me and say, "Man, it's amazing how God is using you," and, "You inspire me," or, "You are a mighty man of God." What they didn't realize is that, yes, when it came to ministry, when it came to my calling, when it came to me as an individual, I was very strong. However, there was a breach between me and my family. It was time for me to find another mentor. I truly believe that my wife and I wouldn't have made it if would not have found another mentor during that season.

In November of 2007, my family and I were driving to California. My wife and kids were in the back seat enjoying themselves. They were telling stories, loving life, laughing, and having a great time. While driving, I suddenly noticed that I wasn't familiar with most of the stories they were telling. I felt like an outcast. How could I have been in the house with them for all these years and not know what they were talking about? My heart was drawn to the back seat, but I had to consciously strain to keep my eyes forward. As I listened to their voices, the lines on the road began to blur as my tears fell like heavy rain down my cheeks. I felt alone. I felt like a failure. I was ashamed of what I had become. I had a music album out that was circling around the world, I was traveling, doing ministry and motivational speaking just like I had always dreamed. Our bills were paid, and I was serving my country. Those stories and the tears that came as a result of realizing that I had checked out on my family are forever etched in my memory. I realized in that moment, that while all the things I was doing qualified me as a success, I was actually failing in one of the most crucial ways. I was failing as a husband. I was failing as a father. I was failing as a leader and as a mentor.

My mind started replaying all the times my son asked me to play basketball and I would say, "No, daddy's tired. I'll play with you tomorrow." Then I wouldn't play the next day, or the next day, or the next day. I thought about every time my daughter would want to make music with me or ask me to lay down with her before she would go to sleep. I would say, "Daddy is tired. I'll lay down with you tomorrow." Then I wouldn't lay down with her the next day, or the next day, or the next day. It was these thoughts that began tormenting me. It's not that I never did these things, but many times my answer was "not right now." With both hands on the wheel, I was doing everything in my power to not let my family know I was sobbing.

Suddenly, I clearly heard in my spirit that God was giving me a second chance with my family. I felt the relief of knowing that it wasn't over. It wasn't too late for me to take my rightful place as a husband and a father. I could be intentional with my family. From that moment forward, I made a decision that I would include my family in everything I did and that I would put them first.

Upon my return, I called my friend Steve Alexander. Steve is an incredible husband and father. When we had previously been around each other, I had noticed how well he loved his wife and kids, how he served his family, and how he lived so congruently to God. I told him that I needed help. I told him that I was failing as a father and as a husband and that I needed guidance. I asked him to mentor me. He flipped my world upside down by sharing with me the importance of being a husband first, then being a great father to my children. Finally, I had some order in my life. Steve played no games when it came to his wife and kids. That was a balance that I needed in my life because I was working so hard for God, but I was leaving my family behind.

He helped me learn that my first priority was my personal one-on-one relationship with God. Not works, music, ministry, serving at the church, or any of that. He taught me that it was God the Father first. After that, it wasn't family second, but my wife second. This was so key for me! And I'm still benefitting today by understanding that my wife comes after God and before my kids. I know that the world tells us to focus on our kids, but this has caused so many problems in marriages after the kids are gone and out the house. When he taught me this, the stress in my life decreased and the relationship with my family was rekindled. I learned that God, my wife, and my kids, were more important than my professional career or my calling.

Another result from having multiple mentors is that it will expand your network. Whenever you have a mentor, that mentor will bring you into their world. You are then introduced to their top five influences, which expands your network. Now you're not only hearing from your mentor, but you're also getting to hear their mentors who are the people that have a voice in their life. This helps you better understand your mentor, which in turn helps you better understand the things they are telling you. I can't tell you how many times I've benefited from my mentors' networks. My mentors' networks, in a sense, became my network as well. This is vital to maximizing the potential in your life. I can't tell you how many mentors you should have, but I can tell you that it's better to have more than just one. Be careful, though, to put a cap on how many mentors you have because you want to be intentional with all of them.

At times, you may even be mentored from afar. You may have a desire to be a cook, author, actor, actress, or a preacher and love how great someone is in that specific area. So, you spend time studying them and keeping up with them. If this is the case, you can't be intentional with them because you don't have access to them. And that's okay. It's possible to be mentored by someone from afar. It's not a two-way street, but you're constantly soaking up whatever information you can find from them. Nothing is wrong with that at all but remember it doesn't count as a personal mentor. A personal mentor is a two-way street and much more valuable than being mentored from afar.

The question you have to ask yourself is, with the mentors that I have right now, am I hitting every area of my life that needs to be addressed? I challenge you to write down ten areas of your life that need to be discussed, touched on, or opened up to someone else. If you get multiple mentors, they can touch all ten parts of your life that need to be addressed or spoken into. You can hear multiple viewpoints on what you're dealing with. You can get multiple perspectives on your goals and your desires to help you formulate a plan and have a better understanding of where you are headed.

I'm sure you feel there are times in your life where you're dealing with a lot and carrying a lot of weight. Who are you talking to? Who are you venting to? Who are you seeking help from? Are you doing life alone, or are you opening your life up to good people that can help you? There is so much value when we do life together!

THINK ABOUT IT.

Chapter 5

EXPANDING YOUR NETWORK

In the last chapter, we briefly talked about your mentor and their network. Whenever you have a mentor, you usually have a close, personal relationship with them. They pass on to you anything that they have gained and learned. Now that's a great benefit! Listening to your mentor can prevent you from bumping your head on a wall because they've already bumped their head on the same wall and more.

In my mid-twenties, I remember yearning for wisdom, knowledge, and understanding. I made it a point to sit down with men who were anywhere from ten to fifty years older than me. At that age, I was completely on the struggle bus. I had no clue which way was up or down. I had tons of leadership qualities but no direction or guidance. I'm forty-three now, and sometimes I'm still on the struggle bus; however, I have enough wisdom not to get on the bus alone. During this time, I found myself having enough wisdom to surround myself with other men that had already been down the pathway of where I was headed.

I knew there was a particular pathway for my life, but while on that pathway, I would encounter several things. When this happened, I would reach out to my mentors. What came to my surprise was how willing and open these gentlemen were to pour into my life. If I did not ask them, they wouldn't have done it. But because I asked, it gave them a sense of appreciation where they willingly opened up their life to me. You'd probably be surprised at who's willing to spend time with you. Many are just waiting to be asked.

During this time, it sped up the growth in my life. I'm so thankful I was able to recognize the deficiencies in my life and quickly grab mentors to help me walk through the growing pains. Everyone's life is different. However, I believe that we can learn and take a little bit from everyone that we sit down with.

Because my parents were divorced, a lot of my frustration stemmed from that. I didn't quite know how to be a good husband or father. Truthfully, I sucked at it. But it was because I was lacking a blueprint or an example of how to be the best husband and father that I could be. When I sat down with my mentors, who had so much more wisdom than me, I took a little bit, or sometimes even a lot, from each of them. I am here to tell you that was one of the best decisions I ever made in my life.

This is something that should inspire and encourage you. Whenever you talk to your mentor, you are adding to your life each time. Not only that, you also get a piece of everyone that has touched that mentor's life from their childhood up until that very moment you're sitting down with them. So, if they've had five, ten, fifteen mentors who have poured into their life, you receive the summary of all of them. That's the benefit you get from that one mentor. The mentors I mentioned in chapter four had nothing to do with my professional life. It was strictly about my personal life and how I grew personally.

Let's think about this. Just like you, your mentor has a story. They have a story of triumphs, failures, and heartbreak. From divorce, father issues, unemployment, anger, or relationship issues. Perhaps they've had a successful business, successful ministry, or successful marriage. In all these things, your mentor is carrying an expertise in one or many areas.

In my mid-twenties, I was so full of myself and thought I knew it all; but once I surrounded myself with other people, I quickly learned how ignorant I was in many areas. I am not sure I would have realized that if I didn't surround myself with solid people. To tell you the truth, at one point in time, your mentors were also ignorant in several areas. But through life, through pulling themselves up and grabbing other mentors, they were able to become knowledgeable in that area. Now they're passing that down to you. That is one of the benefits of having a mentor.

The definition of benefit is an advantage or profit gained from something or someone. You get an advantage in life whenever you surround yourself with a mentor. That mentor is pouring everything that they know into you. That, my friend, is a great benefit. Let's say you have a desire to start a business, and you have a mentor that is guiding you in the area of this particular business. Your mentor can share with you all the right and wrong things they did. That could save you time, stress, money, and heartache. It can even keep you from wanting to quit because this mentor has been through every level that you've been through. You can learn from their successes and failures.

Because you are connected to this mentor with this business, they also have a network of people that they connect with. Whenever that mentor goes to a conference or something local happening in your area, your mentor may bring you along with them. You get to meet everyone that's in this same area of focus as you. Then boom, your network has now expanded! Relationships and who you know is everything. Because your mentor brings you into his circle in that particular area, you are immediately ahead of any person that walks up to that person for advice. Your mentor endorsed you and because of the connection, whoever that mentor is connecting you with automatically feels more comfortable. They know that if they're introducing you to them, you must be someone that they're willing to vouch for.

The relationship with your mentor has now produced a new relationship for you. Although your mentor may know a lot about the area of business that you're interested in, the person they're connecting you with may know things your mentor doesn't. That is increasing your knowledge of understanding in the area that you are working in. That is increasing your network.

An example of this happening in my own life was with Dad and Mom Stovall. Dad Stovall was one of the men that I would sit down with and immerse myself in his knowledge and his wisdom. I loved sitting at his feet.

My marriage was horrible in the beginning years. I was not a proper husband and father, and I didn't have direction on what to do or how to do it. My wife and I started spending time with the Stovall's. They were the most coveted couple in our church. Dad Stovall stood six foot five inches tall, and his heart was the size of any room he stepped into. Mom Stovall so gracefully blessed us with her presence. When she moved across a room, it looked like her feet didn't even touch the floor. Together they created an unstoppable dynamic duo. We were blessed that they pulled us into their circle and became our marriage mentors. The way he treated his wife, his queen, blew me away! I had never seen a man treat his wife the way Dad Stovall treated Mom Stovall. He was such a gentleman. He opened the door for her, danced with her, and just took great care of her. My wife and I gravitated to them because of this.

The Stovall's had a marriage ministry. After pouring into us for about a year, they brought us into their network. There were six other couples in their ministry. The knowledge and wisdom we were receiving from the Stovall's immediately expanded. Not only did we have one dynamic couple pouring into us; we now had seven because of the other six couples that served with them.

When they brought my wife and I in, the other couples quickly embraced us, and immediately started pouring into us. We started learning things from them and it wasn't always about marriage. Sometimes it was about how to have fun as a family, ways of putting your family first, and order of life. Other times it was showing me ways to have daddy and daughter time or father and son time. Before then, I didn't know anything about these things.

This is an example of where mentors brought us into their network of people, and we benefited immensely. At that time, that was my greatest need. My greatest need wasn't money or my professional career. My greatest need was that I needed help in being the priest, provider, and protector of my home. The Stovall's opening up their network to us was one of the best things that ever happened, and I believe this saved our marriage. This is an example of what I mean when I say that your mentor matters, and their circle matters, and that you can benefit from their circle.

You also need to expand your mind beyond money,

professional career, or anything pertaining to self-gain. What does it matter if we attain greatness in our professional career but lose everyone around us? There are many lonely people at the top. Professional career and money are important, but I'm speaking to your innermost being right now. Strip away the accolades, and what do you have? This is why I say network outside of just your professional career. I'm talking about building your network so you can grow in wisdom, character, humility, mental, emotional, and physical health just to name a few. Build your network in what books to read, because if your mentor is a book reader, they can tell you what books impacted their life. They can let you know what motivational speakers have made a difference in their lives. They can share with you which TV shows helped develop their mind in certain areas. You automatically benefit from everything that influences your mentor because they are pouring into you. Remember, it's not so you can be their clone. All these things help build you up to be the best version of yourself.

It all goes back to the question, why do life alone? Why continue to bump your head against the wall or find things out the hard way? That is a form of pride. Humility says you do not know it all and still have things to learn. Humility says you need to surround yourself with great people. You do that so you can grow. The benefits of surrounding yourself with good people and having a mentor in your life is it expands your value, your relationships, your knowledge base, and who you can go to for various things in your life.

A mentor brings you in and develops you. They help you maximize your potential. Once you have established trust, they will introduce you to their connections. You can't expect a mentor to connect you with their circle immediately. It takes time. It's not just on the mentor to give. As a mentee, it's important that you reciprocate and show them appreciation for them pouring into you. You do that by making sure you show up when they ask you to show up, be on time, and you follow through with any tasks that they give you.

As Nick and I were building a relationship and worked on music together, he saw my consistency. I finally got to the level where Nick felt comfortable opening up his network. Because Nick had been traveling for ten years, he already had connections all over the world. When he pulled our group into that circle, our music exploded, and ministry opportunities were immediate. We were a rap group that quickly took over our city and surrounding area. We became national recording artists and started traveling all across the country.

Things would not have happened at that speed if we didn't have the benefit of Nick having all the connections, having a large network in the music arena, and knowing what to do. And it wasn't just about the music. It was knowing how to conduct yourself when you're around people, what traps to watch out for, how to handle business, and how to build relationships.

Nick was able to shape us because he had the experience that allowed us to have the character to be able to travel and show our gifts and our talent. We were able to maintain those open doors because he poured into our character by mentoring us; and we grew in leaps and bounds. Because of his network, we were already ahead of the game. That's an example of a mentor pulling you into their network. It speeds up the process. As a result of a mentor allowing you into their network, whatever dream or goal you have is expedited. You benefit in the end by reaching your goal faster. How can you begin expanding your network today?

THINK ABOUT IT.

_____

_____

_____

_____

_____

_____

_____

_____

_____

_____

_____

_____

_____

_____

_____

_____

_____

_____

Chapter 6

THE IRON SHARPENING PROCESS

As a kid, I absolutely loved going to the country. Some of my fondest memories are of hanging out with my grandparents and living the country life. When I say country, there's no city close and nothing but dirt roads to travel on. The closest town was about eight miles away. The house was maybe 700 square feet, but at the time it felt so much larger than that because of the love. Every holiday our large family of 100 people or more would gather there, and we never complained about space. No central heat or air. We just had a fan in the windows for when it was hot and a cast iron wood burning stove for when it was cold. When it was hot, it didn't matter if you were outside or inside. The temperature was about the same. When it was cold outside there was a huge difference between outside and inside. My grandfather had it so hot in the living room that the devil couldn't even stand it. My brothers and I used to see who could stand the longest in our underwear by the stove. Afterwards you had to sit down immediately with those tighty whities burning your buns. The cast iron stove worked amazing, but it took hard work to keep it going. My grandfather would often ask me if I wanted to chop wood with him. I was always up for the challenge. It was my opportunity to show my grandpa how much of a man I was. We would go out next to his shed, but it took me a year or so to recognize my grandfather's pattern.

Since I was a young boy wanting Paw Paw's approval, I would be eager to show him what I was made of. I would beat him to the shed and grab the first axe available. I knew one method was swing, swing, swing. But I'd tire myself out trying to chop the wood. My grandfather, on the other hand, would sit down, take a piece of iron, and stroke his axe before swinging it. He didn't glance up or say anything to me. In the beginning, I never knew why he would waste so much time sitting down striking the axe instead of striking wood. My thinking was ignorant. I figured whoever got the most swings would produce the most firewood. Not for Paw Paw. He took his time sharpening his axe.

Once he finally started chopping wood with me, it was like a hot knife going through butter. Seems like every time he swung the wood would split. It even sounded differently when he would hit the wood. I would get so mad and frustrated. I knew I was as strong as my grandfather. After all, he was getting older. I couldn't understand how he was busting up the wood so much faster than I was. I eventually learned that my grandfather got a kick out of watching me try to chop wood with a dull axe. The term work smarter not harder did not apply to me. I may have been as strong as my grandfather, but I wasn't as wise as him. I am sure my grandfather must have learned his wisdom from Abraham Lincoln who said, "Give me six hours to chop down a tree and I will spend the first four sharpening the axe."

Eventually, my grandfather would give me his axe. Then when I chopped, I would feel like I was as strong and as accomplished as he was. I learned that it wasn't about the strength. It was about the technique and how sharp the iron was.

Figuratively speaking, your mentor teaches you how to make an axe. They show you how to create the handle, how to fashion the shape of the iron by putting it through the fire, and then how to craft the head of the axe. The mentor shows you how to hold the axe and also the correct technique for swinging it. But none of that matters if you're using a dull axe. As you can see by my example, you can go through the entire process and accomplish very little if your axe is dull.

Think about this from a life perspective. Essentially, that's what a mentor does for your life. A mentor can help speed up the process and allow you to learn things much faster. Even something that would normally take you years or even a lifetime to learn can be learned or accomplished at a much faster rate by simply having a mentor. You'll waste much less time trying to figure out these things in life.

This level of mentorship is where you need your friends, your buddies, your circle. These are the people that are parallel to you...eye, heart, and mind level. You can wrestle, you can fight, and you can learn how to defend why you feel the way you feel. You can hear others' perspectives. These are your peers. These are your circles.

I love this because at this stage, you can be brutally honest and question your friends about why they feel the way they feel and vice versa. From a mentor's perspective it's more about listening and sometimes less engagement. But during the iron sharpening level, this is where you can fuss and fight. You can explain why you feel the way you feel. You can discuss your mentor's perspective on a matter, and then you can question and challenge that perspective.

While going through this process, the iron is being sharpened. There can be a lot of friction and you can get tired. Your mentor is someone that you look up to and that pours into you. But this second level is just as important as the first level. This level in your life helps create your "why." Why do you think the way you think? Why do you feel the way you feel? Why are you doing what you're doing in life?

The people at this level challenge you on a whole different level than your mentor. You still have honor and respect for your mentor, but this level right here is where you get dirty. This is where you cry. This is where you regurgitate the things that you've heard, and allow your peers to challenge you by giving you their perspective. Their perception is not meant to change your mind. But to prove that the better you understand what's being given to you, the better mentor you will become for someone else.

You usually spend more time with your peers and the people in your sphere of influence at this level than you do with your mentors or your mentees. These are the people that you have fun with. These are people that you're brutally honest with and they are brutally honest with you. You are essentially mentoring each other. I compare it to being in the military. In the military, you have many people with different ideas about life and different personalities, but you have a common goal. You may fight and yell at each other, you may have your differences, but the aim is to accomplish the overall goal for the platoon versus your own ideas.

When you are sharpening your iron with your peers, you may have some very intense arguments but you both have the same goals. I'm not talking about everyone in your life that you come into contact with. These are your brothers and your sisters that you're doing day-to-day life with. These are the ones that you talk to all the time and that you hang with. Just like the iron sharpening process, sparks will fly, and other people will see those sparks fly. Other people will see how you swing the axe and will judge you. You know, though, at the end of the day that when you get done with this iron sharpening process, you are going to be able to attack your goals faster than you would have been by yourself.

Why do life alone? No matter how pure the iron is, you can't sharpen it yourself. No matter how great your technique is or how strong the handle is, you can't sharpen it yourself. A tool cannot become sharper without the presence of another tool. Who are the tools in your life? Who is sharpening you?

If you try to sharpen yourself and your iron with rock, metal, or steel, you can cause damage. Remember, this circle I'm referring to are like-minded people that have some of the same goals as you. They are people who can build you up instead of tear you down. When you surround yourself with these people, that's how you sharpen yourself.

The iron sharpening process brings a great level of accountability because they're in your inner circle; they know what you have going on. The door is open for them to ask how you are doing in different areas of your life and to question whether you got certain tasks done. These are the people that you are vulnerable with and that you have given permission to bring correction to you. If you trust them enough to open up to them, this means that you have given them permission to give you their honest opinion about whatever it is you are discussing.

I remember when I first came into the faith I had absolutely no accountability. All the friends that I had were doing the opposite of what I wanted to do. In a sense, I had iron, but I wasn't able to sharpen myself with the friends that were in my circle. It was like trying to use rock to sharpen my iron. It's impossible to sharpen iron using rock, and eventually you damage the iron and yourself.

I eventually surrounded myself with some godly men on my level. My life changed greatly when I surrounded myself with like-minded people and people that I could sharpen myself with. When you're doing life alone, you feel like you're the only one going through your situation and that no one could possibly understand what you're going through. That brings a lack of confidence, a lack of direction, and possibly even depression. When I found out from other godly friends that I wasn't the only one going through what I was going through, it actually inspired me and gave me hope. They helped me to see that I wasn't the only one feeling the way I was. They were able to tell me how they felt and how they made it through certain situations and difficulties in life. They were able to explain how a mentor guided them through how to pray, how to fast, and how to read the Bible. That inspired me and played a major role in who I am today.

During this time in my life, I didn't have a mentor. I had people I could learn from that I was walking through life with and was sharpening my iron with. If you're swinging with a dull axe you may eventually get to your goal, but it will take you so much longer. I needed a mentor. You need a mentor, and you need peers in your life that will help sharpen you.

The Bible says in Proverbs 27:6, "Faithful are the wounds of a friend." During the iron sharpening process, you're vulnerable so your friends can see inside your life. They may tell you things that you don't want to hear or things that may offend you; but you can go home, process, and remember that it is coming from your friend. You can remind yourself that the iron sharpening process doesn't always feel good, but it's necessary. It's not just about you. You're not the only one benefiting. You are helping to sharpen another person in the process of being sharpened yourself. You are helping another person to reach their destiny and their maximum potential. That's a Kingdom mindset! And that's how we make the world a better place.

THINK ABOUT IT.

_____

_____

_____

_____

_____

_____

_____

_____

_____

_____

_____

_____

_____

_____

_____

_____

_____

_____

Chapter 7

PAY IT FORWARD

We've all heard the phrase "pay it forward" before. It's an expression for when a recipient of an act of kindness does something kind for someone else. We have all probably benefited at some point in our life from someone paying it forward. Most likely if you have a mentor, that's exactly what they are doing. Someone was a blessing in their life and helped guide and shape them. They realized the benefit of it and said, "Why would I not help someone else benefit from having a solid, consistent voice in their life?"

Our society nowadays is all about me, myself, and I. What can *I* do to gain a leg up? How can people help *me*? What is *my* potential? How can I maximize *my* life? We must realize that life is not just about us. Life must be about asking how we can help those around us. As my good friend, Andre Daughty, says, "When one wins, we all win."

A great example of the pay it forward principle is displayed in a video entitled *Ripple*. In the story, a young lady was at the grocery store with her brother and grandmother, and she wanted to get something special for her grandfather who was at home. After deciding on a special cake, they went to pay for their items. However, they didn't have enough money to purchase the cake and decided to put it back. The young lady was very disappointed as the family took their groceries and left the store. A gentleman behind them in line purchased the cake and quickly caught up with them outside.

He tried to give the cake to the young lady, but the grandmother said they could not accept it. He explained that when he was seven, his mother wanted to buy him a birthday cake; but they didn't have enough money to buy the one he wanted. Standing by them was an older gentleman that overheard. He bought the cake and gave it to him, telling him, "Here, have the cake. Happy birthday!"

He went on to say he had never forgotten about the man in that grocery store line. After listening to this explanation, the grandmother accepted the cake. She asked for his contact number in order to repay him once they had the money. He wrote on a small piece of paper and leaned down in front of the young lady that originally wanted the cake and said, "Promise me something. Someday when you're able to help somebody, you will do it?" The young lady shook her head yes, and he handed her the piece of paper he had written on. When the grandmother asked for his name, he responded, "I'm the man who was in line behind you."

When they returned home, the young lady excitedly gave the cake to her grandfather explaining she picked it out for his birthday. The grandfather proceeded to tell the grandmother she shouldn't have spent the money on a cake. She explained that a kind man actually paid for it. The little girl then handed her grandfather the piece of paper the man had given to her, saying, "He gave me this note."

As the grandfather read the note that was given to him, he recalled a time many years earlier when he had purchased a cake for a small boy in a grocery store. He had written the exact same thing on a piece of paper and handed it to that little boy. That's when he realized that the gentleman that purchased the cake for his family that day was the same little boy that he had bought the cake for all those years ago.

The phrase written on both notes read, "A simple act of caring creates an endless ripple that comes back to you." In an act of kindness many years ago, the grandfather purchased a cake for a young man. That young man didn't forget this kindness and paid it forward years later by purchasing a cake for a young lady, who just happened to be the granddaughter of the man that had shown him so much kindness before. This is a beautiful story.

Let's dive into this ripple concept a little deeper. Whenever there is a body of water, one single drop can create a ripple that can last a long time. One drop of caring can last a long time. One drop of love can last a long time. One drop of confidence can last a long time.

You see, whenever you mentor someone, you're not only impacting that specific person. You're also impacting everyone that they are connected to, including their spouse, their kids, their extended family, their friends. There's a bigger picture. You are impacting their next generation that may not even be alive yet. That is the gift that keeps on giving.

It's important that we understand the principles of giving. The note from the story said that an act of caring comes back to you. It can come back to you in various forms. It may be an act of kindness shown to you later. It could be an act of kindness shown to someone in your family. When you are kind to others, when you pour into others, when you mentor others, that is paying it forward. It is the law of the land that when you give, it will be given back to you.

I am a product of being mentored. I am a product of someone else paying it forward. Because someone paid it forward, I can boldly tell you that the relationship between me and my son is better. Someone else took the time to pour into me to make sure that I was the best young man possible and I'm so thankful that they paid it forward.

When you've been mentored and experienced the iron sharpens iron process, it should tug on your heart to help someone else. Because you have reaped the benefits of someone helping you, it's imperative that you help other people. You may be thinking that you are not qualified. Let me tell you though that you *are* qualified to help other people. Naturally, we think that we need to have a lot of money or own a business to help someone else. We may even think we have to be famous or have all kinds of accolades to mentor someone. I'm here to tell you that is a lie!

Think about this. There is organized crime, mafias, and gangs throughout the country and world. The leaders in these groups are mentoring the next and current generation after them. They are using their influence in a negative way, but they are still mentoring the next generation to carry out the traditions of the gang. If a gang member can mentor another gang member, why can't you, a good yet imperfect person, mentor someone else?

You may not be great in all areas of your life, but there is something that you do, and you do it well. If you keep that to yourself and don't pass it on, you will feel unfulfilled at some point in your life because you didn't pass along your knowledge. You, my friend, are qualified to mentor. All it takes is a caring, loving, a willing heart, and a desire to help someone else.

Mentors are needed on all levels. Someone may need guidance in their professional career. Another may need tips on being a husband or father. Perhaps someone is getting married or going through a divorce. Maybe they've become stagnant in their life and need help moving forward. Someone may want to write a book or learn how to be a professional fisherman. Another may be interested in learning more about art or how to work on a car. It doesn't always have to be something deep. Let that sink in. It doesn't have to be serious or a life or death situation. Mentors are needed on all levels and in many areas.

The truth is there are plenty of people walking this earth that have no clue that they need a mentor. You've already been mentored yourself or will soon be mentored. You have an understanding that everyone needs a mentor. If you've been mentored before or are currently being mentored, survey your sphere of influence. Consider your home, your job, a family member, your neighborhood. Think about those around you that can benefit from having a consistent voice in their life.

Sometimes the idea of mentoring can be intimidating. The thought of being responsible for another person is scary. We think it's a lot of weight to carry, and it's our fault if they mess up. We may think we have to always be available to them and make them our priority. If you're thinking this way, let me free you of those notions.

I like to think of mentoring like a pinball machine. The ball is waiting for something to push it so it can explore territory that it's never been to before. The mentee is the ball, and the push is you. Once the mentee is pushed, it's now exploring new territory and going wherever it wants to go. You don't decide where it goes. You don't decide what it hits or what wall it bounces off of. You don't determine how high or how low it goes or how many points it gets. None of that is your responsibility. I think of the mentor as the bumpers on the side. You let the ball, the mentee, roam wherever it wants to go. If they get too far to the left or to the right, you give them a bump, a small push in the right direction, so they can start exploring again.

Free yourself of thinking that you are responsible for them. If you're mentoring someone and they make a really bad decision, even one where they end up in jail, that is not your fault. Your mentee is the one that made the decision that ultimately landed them in jail. You gave them the tools and helped them walk through life. They just made a choice to make a bad decision. That bad decision is not a reflection of you.

If you're holding back from having a mentee because you feel that you're already responsible for enough people, including your family, don't. You are not responsible for your mentee. A mentor is simply someone that shares their knowledge and wisdom with someone else to help them stay on the pathway that has been created for them. It's ultimately up to the mentee to decide what to do with that information.

Being a mentor is a friendship where you bring another person in close, allowing them to see your wounds.

You allow them to see your growth, your success, and your failures. You encourage them to overcome life's struggles and shoot for the stars. You may not be best friends or even hang out with them all the time, but you can still play a major role in their life. Mentoring relationships vary. There's no absolute right or wrong way as long as you are being intentional with the time that you do have with them. A level of respect should be there as well. You are friends, but there's still a level of honor that needs to come from the mentee to the mentor.

Your life should be an open book where you share things with your mentee. But you also have to use wisdom and know how to articulate to them the different parts of your life, especially ones where you experienced growing pains. You don't want to do it in a way where you're giving them a green light to go do whatever they want. You need to present it in a way that shows them what your challenges were and how you made it through.

Sometimes as a mentor, your job is just to be. Just be. That means to just be whatever they need. Some people don't need or want a ton of guidance, assignments, or another leader. They may be doing well for themselves, already have their life mapped out, or have other voices of reason in their life. Everything may be going well and what they need is someone to just be a friend. Just be a listening ear. Just be that person they can go grab a bite with and bounce things off of. Just be that positive person in their life. Just be.

THINK ABOUT IT.

Chapter 8

HOW DO I MENTOR?

In the military we had a unit called the military intelligence. Their job was to collect as much data as possible. They would gather information, and then provide guidance and direction on how a situation should be approached and handled. Military intelligence and mentoring aren't the same thing, but the approach can be the same. In a sense, you're collecting as much data as you can as a mentor. That way you can better assist your mentee in order to put them on the correct pathway.

Many times, we like to talk to hear ourselves, but you can't make a lot of movement with your mentee if you're doing all the talking. How can you know what they're facing and fully dealing with if you never listen? How can you collect the data that's needed to make an analysis and a plan to be the best mentor possible if you're the only one talking? You do this through active listening and simply doing life with them.

I believe it is almost impossible to be a good mentor to someone else if you've never been mentored yourself. How can you know how to do something that you've never been a part of? You develop your personal blueprint on how to mentor someone else through the process of being mentored. This blueprint isn't set in stone because every mentor and mentee are different. However, if you've never been mentored before, it is really hard to know how to handle situations, to know what to do and what not to do. Because of this, I highly suggest that you go through the process of being mentored before you take on a mentee.

If you get a flat tire and you've never changed one before, you can probably figure it out and change the tire by yourself. However, that will come with a cost because it will take you longer. Much of your time will be spent trying to figure out how everything works. You may even have to make a phone call to get directions to accomplish changing the flat tire. Suppose, though, that someone showed you how to change a tire. Think about how much more confidence you would have if you get a flat tire knowing that you've been taught how to change it.

It's the same thing with mentoring. You may be able to mentor if you've never had a mentor, but you may not reach your maximum potential as a mentor if you've never been shown how to be mentored. You're not going through the process of being mentored to duplicate it, but to help you develop your own pattern.

As a mentor, I have something that I like to call structured time and unstructured time. Both are equally important. Structured time is where you are very intentional.

You have a plan or an idea, and you know what you're going to talk about. It's a little more intense. This is when you are up in their Kool-Aid as the saying goes. Basically, all up in their business. You're very direct with them about what's happening in their life. Unstructured time is when you are just spending time with your mentee having fun. This could be fishing or hunting together, grabbing a quick lunch, or really whatever it is you both like to do.

I know unstructured time is fun, but it's actually one of the most important processes of being a mentor. Unstructured time is where you listen and learn about your mentee. You learn what they love and what they hate. Through normal conversation you're able to find out what things they're dealing with at the time. It is through this unstructured time that you are able to determine the topics to discuss during your structured time.

If there is not trust between a mentor and a mentee the relationship will not thrive. That trust is built during the unstructured time. There are different ways you can build trust, and one of the ways is being intentional with your mentee. That means spending time with your mentee while limiting outside distractions such as cell phones or bringing other people along who may take your attention away from them. When a person knows that you set time in your busy schedule for them in order to be what they need in their life, the door to their heart is opened and they allow you in.

Another way you gain trust is by being transparent, open, and honest about your own shortfalls in life. When a mentee knows that you're real and willing to open up your book of life to share your failures as much as your successes, it builds trust. The mentee realizes that you're human, just like them; and if you're willing to talk about your shortcomings, they're more willing to open up and talk about their shortfalls. Think about it. If you never share your challenges with them, you can't expect them to share their challenges with you. As you share your mistakes, their level of respect for you will increase. During this unstructured time, you're simply doing life together and getting to know one another. Don't put pressure on yourself to think that you have to learn everything about each other in one session. It takes time.

If I have an orange, there are many ways I can get to the fruit on the inside. One way is to squeeze it and force the fruit out. When I squeeze it, I can still retrieve the fruit; but a lot of it will be left inside the peel. However, if I take my time to slowly peel the outside away from the fruit, I'm left with a full orange. This is the same with your mentee. You need to gently peel back the layers of their life. There are layers to everyone, including you and your mentee. You'll need to gently pull back the layers of your mentee, which may take some time. Do not be discouraged by any resistance, or if it seems like your mentee is holding back. Remember the first time you were mentored. You didn't spill your guts about everything you were dealing with the first time you sat down with your mentor. It took time for you to trust them before you opened up. The same thing applies to your mentee, and it's going to take time for them as well.

Every mentee is different and not every person is mentored the same way. As you're developing your mentoring blueprint, you can't have just one plan for everybody. People have different personalities and priorities and are at different levels in their life. During the unstructured time is how you develop your game plan as a mentor.

Keep in mind throughout the entire mentoring process that you can't have your own agenda. You can't go into it thinking you're going to do it this way or that way because this or that way worked for you. Duplicating yourself should not be the goal here. This man or woman, boy or girl, are on their own pathway. If you go in with the mindset of duplicating yourself, then you are completely failing your mentee. There's nothing wrong with inspiring them and telling them some of the things you did to get to the level of success you have. However, you have to remember that they are an individual and God has created them to be uniquely who they are.

You also have to remember that you are a resource, not *the* source. You can't build them up to depend exclusively on you because you are a human being, and you will fail them. If you build them up to solely depend on you, you are short-changing your mentee. Their source has to be

God because He is the only one who will not fail them. If you build yourself up as a god in their eyes, when you make a mistake, and you will make a mistake, you can completely destroy the foundation of their life. Point them to their pathway, point them to their greatness, point them to their destiny, and ultimately, point them to God.

Structured time has some similarities to unstructured time. It is highly relational, and you have to be intentional. When you are with your mentee, they have to feel like they are your number one priority in that moment. When I'm with my mentee, the only time I disengage is if my wife or children call me. Outside of that, I do not answer the phone. Structured time is a little more intense than unstructured. Unstructured time is where you have fun and get to know each other. Structured time is where you come with the plan you developed from the data you collected during the unstructured time. Your plan allows you to know the best way to lead this person as a mentor.

As a mentor in the structured time, you are giving your mentee the tools to help them build their life. Remember, it's up to them to do the building. Your job is to give them the best tools you have so they can build the areas they're weak in. You may not even provide all the tools needed since you may not be their only mentor. You may be one of many sources they rely on. Structured time takes preparation and planning. You need to have a goal when working with your mentee, one that is best for them. Mentoring someone isn't always easy. It can be intense at times and requires strong accountability. As a mentor, you have to be willing to hold not only your mentee accountable, but yourself as well.

Don't shy away from giving your mentee assignments. An assignment may be reading a book, committing more time to God, working harder on their job, or listening to a motivational speaker. If they are struggling in the area of being intentional with their family, you can ask them to set a time dedicated to their children every evening for the next week. Giving the assignment is just part of the process. You also have to follow up. From time to time my mentors give me assignments. If I don't carry out those assignments, my mentors will correct me. That's called accountability. You cannot successfully mentor without accountability. Oftentimes that means giving an assignment and following up to make sure it is done.

Mentoring is a two-way street. If you're a mentor and give assignments that are never completed, or if you're the only one who ever reaches out, the last thing you want to do is waste their time and yours. Now, mentors, that doesn't mean you give up easily. It may be that your mentee is going through a tough time, and you have to fight through that with them in order to stay engaged. On the other hand, if a pattern is created where there is a breach in your relationship, it may mean that their season with you is over. You have to be mindful to recognize the difference.

This structured time is an investment. Many people know that an investment doesn't always yield rewards. You get out of it what you put into it. That means you will never yield a reward if you don't invest. If you don't prepare or don't remember the things that were discussed previously when you met, how can you invest in your mentee and properly give them what they need?

When we invest our money, we stay on top of it. We watch it to see how the investment is doing and we follow up. From a mentorship perspective, your time is your investment. The more time you invest into your mentee, the better chance you have of yielding a great return. Keep in mind, if it doesn't yield a great return, don't beat yourself up or worry about it. Your job is to protect your investment and be the best mentor that you can be in their life.

Structured time is direct and in your face. It's all about asking questions and gaining more understanding of their life, their relationships, and their career. When your mentee opens up about struggles in their life, that gives you permission to ask about those struggles when you meet in the future. You need to check up on your mentee. It's like a car. If you drive a car and never check up on it, how will you know what's going on or what needs to be worked on? If the warning light is on and you keep ignoring it, then you may find yourself on the side of the road. You must be intentional with checking on your mentee. Don't be afraid to ask the hard questions. Don't be afraid to ask them to share their goals with you. You may be able to help them with their goals. You can also hold them accountable, which is just as important.

Suppose your mentee tells you that one of their goals is to find a job or even get a better job. Your responsibility is to check in on them regularly. Ask questions. Ask them how their search is going. Find out what they're doing to work toward their goal and if they're making any headway. If they haven't, you can gently hold them accountable and bring more encouragement if needed. Being a mentor is a job. Like any job, it's not always going to be easy. Now, I do think it's easier than what some people think, but sometimes you must get in the trenches and dig with your mentee.

I recently did a podcast with Mentor House which was founded by Derrick Sier and Heady Coleman. Mentor House does a live podcast recording about mentoring called Mentor Hour that aims to connect aspiring and seasoned mentors. During the podcast, I was asked a question that made me think about some of the things I do when I'm being intentional as a mentor, things I hadn't put much thought into until I was asked this question. Derrick asked me, "What is your secret sauce?"

Think about when your mom or grandma or favorite uncle cooks that delicious dish that everyone loves. Everyone tries to duplicate the dish, including you, but no one knows how to make it like them. Unless they tell you what's in the secret sauce, it's almost impossible to replicate the dish. You can get close, but it's never quite as good.

I proceeded to tell Derek that my secret sauce is to find out who is in my mentee's circle. If you want to know more about your mentee, find out who the five strongest voices are in their life. This will help you mentor them better, because those five voices are shaping who they are. You can find out very quickly if those voices are fighting for or against the positive things that you're putting in their life.

You can learn so much about your mentee by getting to know the people in their life. You can't be expected to be great friends with these people, but at least knowing them on the surface will help you gather better information on how to mentor your mentee. Your mentee may not share everything with you, especially when they're going through a tough time; but you may get a phone call from someone in their circle because they know that you care for them and are there for them. I had a mentee that I had been mentoring for three years. One day his parents pulled me to the side and told me about some things my mentee was dealing with. My mentee and I were really close. We had a great relationship, but I didn't know that he was dealing with some pretty serious issues. I had no clue he was headed down this path because he would always put his best foot forward for me. If I had not built a relationship with his parents, I would have never known what my mentee was going through. That information was so valuable because between the parents and me, we were able to change the trajectory of this kid's life. Together we were able to help my mentee; but that wouldn't have been possible if I hadn't applied my secret sauce of getting to know the five strongest voices in my mentee's life.

If the person you're mentoring is married, it's imperative that you at least know the spouse at a surface level. Again, you don't have to be best friends with them, but if you're going to be spending time with their husband or wife, it helps if the spouse is comfortable with them being around you. They need to know that you are a positive influence in their life, because if your mentee has to fight their spouse to spend time with you, it could cause a problem in their relationship.

Try your best to always keep your word and your promises when you are mentoring. If you promise your mentee something, it is important that you follow through with that promise. All the time spent with them during unstructured and structured time helps build trust, and that trust can be completely lost if you don't follow through. If you fail to keep your word, be open, be honest, and apologize, or you could lose the respect of your mentee. Don't overlook it as if it didn't happen. Face it and apologize.

While spending time with your mentee, your mindset has to be that you are creating a future mentor. That doesn't have to be the number one thing at the forefront of your mind, but you do need to remember that through everything you do with them during structured and unstructured time. You are not only helping them in areas they need help in and pointing them to their destiny; you are assisting in creating a mentor. Never hesitate to explain to your mentee why you're doing what you're doing. Never hesitate to break down the process of mentoring with them. The whole purpose of being a mentor is to create a mentor that creates a mentor that creates a mentor. It's the gift that keeps on giving!

You have the capacity to mentor. Someone has poured into your life. Now do the same thing with someone else's life. Our world would be a much better place if we would all be selfless and give a piece of our self to someone else.

THINK ABOUT IT.

Chapter 9

FIGHT THROUGH THE RESISTANCE

What is love? The dictionary says it is an intense feeling of deep affection or a great interest and pleasure in something. However, you and I know that everyone's definition of love is different. It is developed in our mind and heart based on our upbringing. And everybody's upbringing is different. Some had a wonderful life: a life with both parents, friends, and little or no struggles. Some grew up in a single-parent home where one parent was never present, went to prison, or possibly even passed away. Others may have been mistreated or suffered abuse at the hands of a family member, whether it be mental, physical, or sexual.

The word love can't be described in one sentence. Whenever we mentor someone, we must remember that their definition of love may be different from our definition of love. For some, loving others is easy; and for some, loving others is hard, or sometimes, in their mind, impossible. So many movies and songs describe what they think love is. As a mentor, you have to be aware that your definition of love may not line up with your mentee's definition of love.

I bring this up because you have to fight through the resistance with some mentees. They may have their guard up. They may have built up a wall for protection. They may not be used to allowing people inside their heart. If you come across this, don't be discouraged. Move at the pace of the mentee.

As a man, we all know the stigma that comes with being a strong man. Little boys don't cry. They don't pout or show emotions. We are expected to be as tough as nails. Because so many people were raised this way, myself included, it's hard to be vulnerable with other people. Being vulnerable is a sign of weakness in our minds, and that wasn't allowed. In fact, many of us got spankings for showing signs of weakness. *Stop crying. Shut up. You have five seconds to hush up or I'm going to give you something to cry about.* These words have shaped so many people.

For some, their mother or father may not have been in their life to show them love. Others may have had a mother or father that was active in their life, but they weren't present. They didn't love on them. In other cases, love has been used to manipulate people. That's why I bring up love and resistance. If your mentee is showing signs of not wanting to open up to you, don't get offended. It takes time. It takes consistency. And remember that being a mentor is an investment, and it may not always yield a return right away.

We all have pride, but that is the last thing a mentor needs to carry on their shoulders. If you go in with the mentality that you don't need to be there or that your mentee should be thankful that you're there, you might as well stop mentoring. Don't get me wrong. There may be a time where things come up and you need to step away from the mentee. If your mentee shows resistance, you must discern between whether it's stony ground or fertile ground. Even fertile ground may have small rocks at the surface, but underneath those rocks is fertile soil. Fight through the rocks to get to the fertile ground beneath.

You have been mentored and have seen the fruits of the process. Your mentee needs you. It doesn't matter the age of the person. They can be young, middle-aged, or older and not realize that they need a mentor. When you come into their life, they may show some resistance because of this. Maybe they've never been cared for before. When you start showing that you care, they may question what you want from them. They may think you have an ulterior motive for wanting to spend time with them.

In the beginning, you don't know their background. They may have been abused or even molested. Maybe they've never been shown love or affection by an adult. Growing up, maybe their mother, father, or grandparent made promises to them and didn't follow through.

My dad is a great man and father. We have a wonderful relationship now; but when I was a child, he really didn't show up for me. He didn't make it to any of my games, my band competitions, or anything that I had going on at church. He just didn't make it to those things. As a young kid, he would give me money when he couldn't make it. I was okay with that, and it made me happy that at least I got money when my father couldn't be there.

However, I'll never forget my freshman year at Langston University. My dad said he was going to come to my game. I had been told this before; but this time I really wanted him there and I thought he was coming. I was devastated after the game when I realized he didn't come. He offered me money like before, but this time it ticked me off. I didn't want the money. I wanted him to show up. I stopped talking to him for a short time after that. I subconsciously held that against my dad for a long time.

As I got older, my dad and I started becoming more intimate as father and son. As we became more intimate, I started learning more about my dad's history and up-bringing, about the things that happened in his childhood and as a young adult. When I learned his story, my heart ached for my dad. My love and grace increased because I now had a better understanding of what formed my dad. I finally understood that my father did the best he could. His capacity to father was limited by his childhood. Once I fully understood that forgiveness came into my heart. I started wanting to be around him more, and those walls I had up with my dad fell away completely. This was all because I learned his story.

You have no idea what your mentee went through as a baby, a kid, a teenager, a young person, or even as an adult. Because of this, you must fight through the resistance. You may not even have a clue what they're currently dealing with. They may be dealing with a possible divorce, lack of finances, or about to lose their house. Perhaps they have bad grades, their father is in jail, or their mother didn't want them. Maybe they're dealing with the loss of a grandparent or another family member. They could feel unfulfilled in life and be dealing with depression and anxiety. You'll never know what they're dealing with if you give up instead of fighting the resistance.

Because I was let down as a child in different areas, my mentor and I had to go through the same thing. I didn't trust men. I didn't trust that they would take care of me or be there for me. My first mentors had to fight through that resistance. I'm so glad that they persevered and saw that I was a damaged young man that just needed to be loved.

Real love can be very intimidating. If you've never experienced real love and someone tries to show it to you, it can be scary. Think about someone who has been injured and is bleeding. The first thing most people do is clean the injury. Even though the cleaning process hurts, it is necessary for the injury to heal. After that, a bandage is placed over the injury. This makes it feel better, but it's difficult for air to get to the wound in order for it to heal. Many people are walking around with a wound with a bandage over it. However, most people know that in order for the wound to heal, the bandage has to come off. A bandage is meant to be temporary to stop the bleeding; but in order for the wound to truly heal, the bandage has to be removed at some point.

It's not an easy process. A lot of times, the wound begins to bleed again once the bandage is removed. It begins to hurt all over again, sometimes worse than when the injury first occurred. To the person that's injured, their pain is real, and you have to respect that. Explain to them why the bandage needs to come off instead of telling them to just suck it up. Let them know that removing the bandage will allow the wound to heal faster.

Throughout this process, keep in mind that there are layers to pain. As you're pulling back the layers with your mentee, some layers are more painful than others. You may get through two layers without difficulty, but when you reach the third layer they may jump out of their seat. Don't let that frighten you. This layer may bring back painful memories, but this is the layer that may need healing the most. It may take longer than other layers; but I guarantee you that once you get past this layer, you'll be able to move on to the next layer. That layer may not be as painful or difficult, but keep in mind that you may hit another layer that will take some time. The dosage of love depends on the level of pain, but you will only know that if you fight through the resistance.

For some, they may not even have an open wound. It may be a bruise instead. A bruise isn't always visible. You can touch someone and when you get to the bruise, they might jump or scream because it hurts when you touch that area. It may bring back terrible memories, and that pain is real to them.

As a mentor, you have to have grace and mercy and recognize that as you're going through these levels with your mentee, they may lash out or try to disappear on you. It makes me think of the movie *Antwone Fisher*.

Antwone Fisher was a troubled kid whose dad was killed before he was born. His teenage mother went to jail soon after, where she gave birth to Antwone. Antwone went into foster care and was placed in a home. Unfortunately, he was severely abused there. He was beaten with wet towels, tied up, called the "N" word on a daily basis, and molested at the age of six. One time he was literally beaten unconscious. He suffered physical, verbal, emotional, and sexual abuse his entire childhood until he finally left the home at the age of fourteen to live on the streets.

This created a very troubled young man. After living on his own for the next few years, he decided to join the U.S. Navy. Antwone was extremely angry and didn't know how to deal with his anger. He got into fight after fight after fight. After so many fights, his commander ordered him to see a psychiatrist, LCDR Dr. Jerome Davenport.

It started out as required counseling, but Dr. Davenport quickly turned into a mentor. For the first time in Antwone's life he was able to talk to someone who cared about him. For the first time in his life, he was speaking with someone who loved him and was willing to fight through the resistance.

It wasn't easy in the beginning. Antwone understandably had his guard up and didn't want to talk much. Eventually, Dr. Davenport fought through the resistance and Antwone started opening up more and more. The more he opened up, the more the anger started rising to the surface. Dr. Davenport could have quit on him, could have decided he bit off more than he could chew; but instead, he hung in there, and layers and layers that had been weighing down on Antwone's shoulders were gradually being pulled back.

Unfortunately, Antwone's required sessions with Dr. Davenport came to an end. One day, he went to Dr. Davenport's office to see him; and when he arrived, the waiting room was filled with other Navy members all waiting to see the doctor. Upon seeing this, his anger rose and quickly boiled over. He began yelling and screaming at the others in the waiting room. Upon hearing the commotion outside his office, Dr. Davenport came out, where Antwone immediately got in his face and continued his yelling. Dr. Davenport called Antwone into his office and immediately checked him. He said, "Do you realize you're yelling at a commanding officer?" This calmed Antwone down for a moment, but the heat was still in his face.

Here was a troubled kid thinking he was going to be abandoned again. Left again. He had finally opened up to someone, and now he wasn't sure if Dr. Davenport would disappoint him like everyone else in his life had. Dr. Davenport was extremely angry at this point. Antwone admitted he messed up, but he wasn't talking about his outburst in the waiting room. He meant that he messed up by talking to and divulging his pain to Dr. Davenport. He now didn't know what to do without his mentorship.

Dr. Davenport could have left it at that. He could have said his job was done, but he didn't. He quickly recognized that he had become more than a psychiatrist. He was a mentor in this young man's life, and Antwone needed him. Dr. Davenport continued being Antwone's mentor, and it completely changed the trajectory of his life. He taught Antwone how to love, how to face his demons, how to move on, and most importantly, how to forgive. He challenged Antwone to go back and find his real mother. Not only did he find his mother, but he went back and faced his abusers, too. He stood at the door and loudly proclaimed, "You tried to kill me. You tried to stop me. But I'm still standing!"

After Antwone faced his giants, he went back to Dr. Davenport. He thanked him for challenging him and for teaching him how to love and how to forgive.

Here's a key part for you to remember as a mentor. Dr.

Davenport told Antwone that he didn't owe him a thank you. He said he was the one who should be thanking Antwone. He went on to explain that when Antwone walked into his life, it blew up his world. He had been dealing with difficulties in his own life when Antwone came into his office. Helping Antwone flip his world right-side up actually helped him. It made him, as his mentor, face his own giants. We all have giants we need to face. Know that when you fight through the resistance and help your mentee, you are ultimately helping yourself.

THINK ABOUT IT.

Chapter 10

ACCOUNTABILITY

Have you ever played darts? Maybe shot at a target with a gun or a bow and arrow? Imagine someone blindfolding you, spinning you around, and expecting you to hit your target. It's pretty much impossible. I would like to see someone do this, but I'm not sure that would ever happen. Many people are walking through life blindfolded, with no direction, and they're trying to hit their target.

I remember being in basic training next to my buddy, Tim, when we were taught how to shoot an M16 rifle. They taught us what to count to while holding your breath, how to aim, and when to fire. Because I grew up in the country hunting and shooting at random things such as bottles, cans, or anything else we use to make our own targets, I was a pretty good shot. But this day almost every single time I rolled my target back to me, there would be less holes than I shot. I was confused because I knew I was a better shot than that, yet somehow my bullets weren't making it to the target.

Meanwhile, my friend next to me had never shot a gun before that day. When we compared our targets, his had multiple shots close to and on the bullseye all the way to the end of the paper, while mine pretty much had no hits. A few here and there. Joking, I asked if he was shooting a machine gun. Both of us were baffled. We knew I should have been a better shot than he was. He was laughing at me while I was getting more and more frustrated.

One of the instructors came over to see what the commotion was. Upon seeing my target, the instructor began to reprimand me. "How are you not hitting the target? We taught you what to do. You need to aim better." I immediately copped an attitude because I knew I was a better shot than the target demonstrated. My attitude was rewarded with push-ups. While I was doing my pushups, the instructor burst out laughing. "Les, I think I know what your problem is. You're shooting at the wrong target." I responded with more attitude telling him that was impossible because I knew what I was doing.

The instructor proceeded to gather my target, my friend's target, and the target on the other side of me. He counted the holes in all three targets. The target next to me had the correct number of holes. My target had far less holes than it should have had, while my friend's target had far too many holes. Logically, he determined that I was indeed an excellent shot hitting bullseye after bullseye, but I was shooting the wrong target. He explained he would allow me to try again to see if I could pass.

I proceeded to explain to my instructor that even

though I shot the wrong target, I should get credit for the shots. My friend's target had multiple bullseyes, and we all knew that was due to my shooting since my friend had never shot a gun before that day. I insisted that I should pass. I protested that I should not have to shoot again.

While I was doing push-ups again for speaking like that, the instructor held me accountable and continued to speak. "What would it look like if I passed you on after you shot the wrong target? I would absolutely be failing you as a leader if I allowed this. As a leader, I must maintain my integrity and hold you accountable so you can be the best airman possible. There are no cutting corners. You either pass or you fail. I'm giving you the opportunity to shoot again. And Airman Thomas, if you decide not to shoot again, you are going to fail."

In that moment of frustration, I learned that hitting the wrong target, even if it's a bullseye, doesn't count. As a mentor, you have to hold your mentee accountable. Let your yes be your yes, and your no be your no. Some like to call it tough love because love is correction. As a mentor, you have the right to love on them through correction. If you see that your mentee is shooting at the wrong target, it is your job as a mentor to try to direct them to the right target.

Growing up, you probably heard the saying, "I do this because I love you," from your parents, your guardians, or maybe even your grandparents. In that moment, you may not have understood what they meant by that; all you knew was that you were receiving correction. It's the same with your mentee. They may not understand it at the time, but at some point, they will recognize that you loved them enough to give them gentle correction to help them aim at and hit the right target. Correction is love.

If you know that your mentee is doing something that is detrimental to his life, harmful to his family, job, or his sphere of influence, it is your responsibility to hear him out. Then, gently bring correction. Of course, you say what you think and give advice; but if they're out of line, it's important that you give correction, because again, correction is love. You can't be a brute about it. You can't be angry and flip tables. You just have to give direction in love.

Your mentee may not always be happy about this, but you have a voice in their life. You are taking time out of your life to be a blessing to them as they're being a blessing to you in return. They will have to learn to be okay with you holding them accountable, because at the end of the day, it's making them a better person.

When you hold your mentee accountable, you're keeping a hand on the pulse of their life. How can you know someone's pulse if you're not close to them? The pulse tells you the beat of the heart. From a mentor's perspective, the pulse is the beat of the mentee's life. What's the rhythm of their life? Is the rhythm consistent or does it fluctuate? Does their rhythm flutter? Has it stopped altogether? As a mentor, it's important to keep your hand on their pulse to see where they're at in life and if anything needs to be done. This will give you invaluable information.

You need to check the temperature of your mentee's life often. No matter how intelligent an individual is, no one can walk into a room and know the exact temperature just by feeling it. It could be freezing, it could be hot, or it could be somewhere in between. Without physically checking the thermostat, there's no way to know the exact temperature.

It's no different with your mentee. You can't look at them and know how they're doing. Looks can be deceiving, attitudes can be misleading, and a happy face can be pretending. Without actually checking, there is no way to know the truth. You check your mentee's temperature by being intentional, talking with them, and finding out what's going on in their life. You have to be able to look beyond what you see and hear in order to check to see what their temperature is.

You can't take their temperature without a thermometer, and your interaction with your mentee is the thermometer. Just as temperatures can change by adjusting the thermostat, you can change a person's life by adjusting your interaction with them. Your mentee may be doing great for several days, but then something can happen to change that. Depending on when you catch them determines their temperature at that time. That's why consistency is important. Meeting with your mentee one time doesn't tell you everything. It may take two times, three times, or possibly even more to get an accurate temperature reading.

Your mentee is human just like you. You have good days and great days. You also have bad days and terrible days. Checking with your mentee consistently over time allows you to know what to set the thermostat at. That's accountability. By knowing your mentee's temperature, you will know what level of accountability they need and can handle. You can only determine this by spending time with your mentee.

Mentorship is a two-way street. The long-term objective is to help your mentee reach their goals, hit the bullseye, maximize their potential, and empower them to be a mentor themselves one day. Through the process, you may be holding their hand at first; but remember, you are not the source. Because you are creating them to be independent, do not handicap your mentee by giving them too much assistance. They may need a lot of help in the beginning, but there's a danger to continuing down that path rather than teaching them to fly on their own.

Think about a baby bird. A baby bird was created and made to fly. Many times, they don't realize this and are content safely staying in the nest. Over time, the mama bird will take care of the baby while it grows stronger and more independent. When the mama bird decides it is time and that the baby is prepared, she will kick it out of the nest. The baby bird will flap their wings and realize they can fly. It's the same with a mentee. They may need a lot of assistance in the beginning, but if you continue to assist them without holding them accountable, without giving them assignments, without teaching them to be independent, you will then start to handicap them. If this happens, your mentee will never learn how to fly on their own.

Keep in mind, mentoring can't be based on your own agenda. It can't be your will for their life. As a mentor, you are simply helping them to be the best person they can be. You have to ask the hard questions. This may make your mentee uncomfortable, but it's important that you do it anyways. You'll find out what the hard questions are through the time that you spend with them.

I recall a time in my life when I was dealing with lust. At this time, Steve Alexander was a strong mentor in my life, and I opened up to him about this. He gave me some assignments to help me with this, and he told me something that I will never forget. He told me not to wait until the fire was hot before coming to him for help. I should go to him when it was only a spark because it's much easier to extinguish a spark than to put out a blazing fire. In fact, he told me not to come him if I wait until it's blazing, and he meant it.

That right there was an example of good old-fashioned

accountability. He didn't beat me up about it or go off on me. He was holding me accountable to tell him before things got out of hand. He gave me other assignments to go along with this, but the very first assignment was to take responsibility to let him know as soon as I began to struggle. By doing this, we could work on my issue while it was still a spark instead of waiting until it became an inferno.

The next time we met up, and the next time, and the time after that, he asked me how I was doing in that area. It may have been uncomfortable for a moment, but it was necessary. To help them get to their destiny, you must help them prevent the crash.

As you give assignments, ask your mentee what their desires and goals are. Find out where they'd like to be in three months, a year, five years. By learning their goals, this gives you direction on how to help them and gives you the right to hold them accountable. One of my goals in 2019 was to read twenty books. I didn't tell my mentors about this goal, and I only made it to six books. If I had told my one of my mentors about this goal, they would have texted me, called me, or asked me about it in our next session. I would have likely gotten closer to completing my goal.

As a mentor, don't allow your mentee to keep their goals to themselves. Specifically ask them what their goals are. You can help them with some of their goals, but some you may not be able to help them achieve. If you can't help them with a goal, that's okay. Don't be hard on yourself and beat yourself up. No one can cover everything. It's impossible. Cover what you can and help them reach the goals that you can.

So many people are walking through life having wreck after wreck because no one has cared for them. No one has shown them love or held them accountable. Most people have the desire to do the right thing, but they just need help. Will you be that person in someone else's life?

THINK ABOUT IT.

_____

_____

_____

_____

_____

_____

_____

_____

_____

_____

_____

_____

_____

_____

_____

_____

_____

_____

Chapter 11

BENEFITS OF MENTORING

As a mentor, your focus should always be on helping your mentee. You should always have a posture of being selfless and knowing that you're in their life to help them. It has to be about them. They are the focus. You need to be intentional and know that you're being used to help them work through hard times, to help them grow, and to challenge them to reach their destiny and maximize potential. It's not about you, it's about the mentee. I want you to think about that as you read through this chapter.

There are definitely benefits to being a mentor. We all want to have a purpose in life. Purpose brings fulfillment, and the simple fact of knowing that you're helping someone else reach their goals and their destiny helps bring a sense of purpose in your life. No matter where you are in life, no matter what age or what profession you're in, when you know that you're helping someone, it brings purpose that leads to fulfillment.

Think about how you love talking about your mentor. If you don't have a mentor, think about how someone you know talks about their mentor. When I talk about my mentors, I light up. I love telling people about the mentors that have helped me in my life. I love highlighting them. I love giving honor to someone who took time out of their life to help me. It makes me feel loved and valued that someone would choose to pour into me.

When you are mentoring and helping someone, think about how you feel when you are honoring your own mentor. One of the benefits of being a mentor is knowing that God is using you to impact your mentee's life in tremendous ways. In the same way you honor your mentor, your mentee will honor you. Being a mentor in someone else's life means you're giving them that same opportunity to feel the excitement of knowing someone is in their life that cares about them. This should bring fulfillment into your life.

Being a mentor gives you a sense of purpose. It doesn't matter what your age is, either. I've especially noticed this with older people. I like to call them seasoned people. Seasoned people have lived a full life. They may be retired and no longer working. They've accomplished many things in their life, but now they may be asking what's next. When you ask a seasoned person to grab a cup of coffee, get something to eat, or when you ask them to mentor you, they often light up. They realize that they have valuable knowledge to share. They realize that life isn't over for them. It gives them purpose.

You will have true fulfillment in your heart knowing

you're giving back and contributing to society. You're leaving a legacy! One of the benefits of being a mentor is that you are adding to your legacy by giving a contribution to society. Not only are you impacting your mentee, but you're impacting their family, their friends, and their sphere of influence. When you help one person be better you are really helping many. That is a large contribution to society.

You are being used to impact someone else's life just like they impacted your life. What contribution will you make to society? What legacy will you leave? How will you be talked about? Will you have people honor you while you're alive? Because I believe in giving people their roses while they are alive, mentees should always honor their mentor and tell them thank you. When this happens, the mentor receives so much joy in their heart because it gives them a sense of fulfillment.

I can't tell you how many times I've sat with a mentee, and while helping them in their life, I recall things that have happened in my own life and how God walked me through it. Speaking with my mentee, I'm reminded of different obstacles I had to climb over and different walls I had to break through. While teaching my mentee, I remember the things in life that I've been through that helped me be the person that I am today. While teaching my mentee, I'm also learning. Sometimes my mentee asks me a question I don't know the answer to. When this happens, I have to Google or research the subject. I'm learning as I do this. I'm teaching it to someone else, and I'm retaining up to ninety-five percent of that knowledge.

Another benefit as a mentor is that it brings accountability to your own life. It makes you reflect on your life and think about the things you're walking through. You may be talking to your mentee about something they're struggling with, whether it be anger, pornography, trust issues, or marriage issues. If you are struggling in any of those areas or any area that's remotely close, it naturally brings accountability in your life knowing that God is using you to help shape the life of another person. How many times have you heard people say that if they could live by the advice that they give others, their life would be so much better? If you're not a mentor, you're not in a position to give advice. However, when you are a mentor, you are able to give advice to others, which will bring accountability into your own life.

At one point in time, I was dealing with anger issues. My mentee came to me about having serious issues with anger. For me, anger has been the main emotion I personally struggle with. I benefitted so much in my own life from helping this young man. Helping my mentee brought accountability into my own life. It helped me to see that I needed to deal with my own anger issues. It caused me to go to my own mentor and be honest with him about what I was dealing with. You would be surprised at how much it helped me resolve my anger issues by talking to my mentee; because when I was speaking to him, I was speaking to myself.

Every person in this world needs accountability in their life, and this increases through mentoring because when you know that you have someone watching you, it makes you want to walk a more upright life. It makes you want to try to be the best husband or wife, father or mother, man or woman that you can be. Your mentee isn't watching for mistakes or to see if you messed up. They're watching you because they look up to you. The more you're involved in someone else's life, the more accountability there is to make sure you're doing the right thing.

There's a quote I once heard Bishop Tony Miller say that I love: "There is no success without successors." Think about all your successes that you've accomplished in your life. What does it really matter if you haven't shared the pathway to your success with a mentee? As a mentor you're not duplicating yourself. However, if you're not passing down to someone else the things you went through to get to where you're at and the knowledge that you've attained, can you really call that success? You may call it a success, but really it is selfish. It's benefiting you, but what good is it if it's not benefiting others? It is vital for us to make sure we have successors. It's important that we impact the next generation by sharing our victories and wins, but also sharing our failures and losses.

You are going to help other people be successful in their life. True leaders create other leaders. Knowing that you're being used to help someone else maximize their life brings satisfaction like no other. Who's coming after you? Who will you pass the baton to? Will you just take the baton with you and not empower others? Here's a quote from Will Smith that I couldn't agree with more. He said, "If you're not making someone else's life better, then you're wasting your time. Your life will become better by making other people's lives better."

Being a mentor aids with personal growth by developing your communication skills and reinforcing study skills. Communication skills are developed while interacting with your mentee. Every person, every mentee, is different. With one mentee you may have to communicate one way, and with another you must communicate another way. This helps you develop your own personal communication skills, how you interact and talk to people, and how you reach them.

Having a mentee allows you to reflect on your own life. Think about where you've come from. Recall all the great things you've done in your life, as well as the hardships you've overcome. Pouring into someone else lets you see that you're not where you used to be. Appreciate where you come from and see that God had His hand on you. I've personally grown leaps and bounds with my mentor but having a mentee has challenged me to grow as a man.

THINK ABOUT IT.

Chapter 12

WALKING IT OUT

In this chapter, I'm going to give you a real-life scenario that displays all three levels of influence being utilized. I had a mentee that had a pretty tough upbringing around gangs and drugs. In fact, he spent some time in prison. Because of his upbringing, his walls were up, and he didn't really trust anyone. I knew that he needed a mentor and some guidance in order to overcome the guilt, shame, and pain of the things that he saw, that he did, and that he went through at an early age.

We became friends and I decided to fight through the resistance. This young man had a lot to offer the world, and I knew that I could help him get to where he needed to be in life. I could help him reach down inside himself and pull out the potential that he had. It took a while for the trust to develop. We had a lot of coffees, lunches, dinners, and just hanging out. We had a few not so pleasant conversations during those gatherings, but it I refused to give up on him. He reminded me so much of myself. He possessed lots of talent and potential hidden deep under all the rubble. I wasn't trying to play God in his life. My role was to start helping him uncover the potential that was already there. We eventually got to the point where we were able to be very transparent with each other through this process.

His transparency grew out of me being transparent about my own life and the different things I went through. I believe as a mentor, in order to get to the next level with your mentee, you must be open and transparent, not only about your victories, but also about your shortcomings and your challenges. You must be willing to expose things that you have dealt with in the past along with any issues you may be currently dealing with.

At some point in our relationship, it became obvious that I was his mentor. Sometimes it happens that way. No official conversation of the title mentor, but you recognize what you are in that person's life. I was spending a lot of time with him, and I could tell that he was dealing with something. Because we had built a relationship, his reaction and posture toward certain things triggered something within me; and I could tell that something wasn't right. After being intentional and spending even more time with him, he eventually felt secure enough to open up to me. He admitted to me that he was dealing with lust. He told me that he wanted to be faithful to his wife. He wanted to walk with integrity and be the man that God had called him to be, but he was struggling with lust in his heart. As he was confessing this to me, he had no idea that I was dealing with the exact same thing. At that time, I couldn't reveal to him that I was also dealing with lust because those sessions had to be about him. In order for me to help him it had to be about him and not me.

In the previous chapter, I talked about how being a mentor brings accountability to your own life. This was exactly the case with me. When my mentee admitted that he was dealing with lust, it struck a chord inside me that I needed to address my own issue. I had not yet spoken to my mentor and admitted this particular struggle, and I came to a realization. How could I successfully be what my mentee needed me to be in his life when I was dealing with the same issue at the same time?

One thing about being a mentor or a mentee is you can't let pride get in the way. I knew I couldn't be prideful and not address my own shortcomings. I didn't beat myself up over it or stop being there for my mentee. I reminded myself that I'm not perfect. There's only one person that's perfect, and that is Jesus. My job as a mentor is to be a reflection of Jesus and to strive to be the best man I can be. Remembering that made me realize that I could still be who I needed to be in my mentee's life, even though my life wasn't perfect. By walking with my mentee through this difficult time in his life, it brought accountability to my own life. I quickly got over myself and remained in the position of helping my mentee, even though I was struggling. Shortly after my mentee talked to me about what he was dealing with, I admitted to myself that it was time for me to face my demons.

I went to my mentor and told him that I was dealing with lust. I had been wrestling with lust by myself. I understood the principle of being transparent and honest with my mentor. However, I let pride and shame stop me from sharing that with my mentor. I'm supposed to be a minister that's living uprightly before God without spot or wrinkle. That way of thinking will cause you to suffer alone because you want to come across as perfect.

Not only that, but I had a real conversation with my wife about what I was dealing with because the lust was attacking me to the point that I was on the verge of doing something that I could not take back. I shared my struggle with my wife because I did not want anything to happen that would change my position as a husband or alter the trajectory of my life by making a mistake. I knew that my wife would war in the spirit with me and stand by me. I needed her to be in agreement with me so I could make it out of this bad situation. My wife did just that and joined me in prayer. God used her along with my mentor to help me walk through the process of overcoming.

At this same time, due to my position in our church, I was counselling other men who were also dealing with lust. I went to my spiritual mentor and let him know what was going on in my life, and he began to walk me through the process of overcoming my issue. He didn't verbally beat me up nor did he ask lots of questions. He allowed me to navigate my own way of sharing because he was concerned with what the next move was. This gave him enough information to guide me through the process.

It's important as a mentor that you do not condemn or beat up your mentee for the mistakes that they make. If you do, your mentee will not be open and honest with you in the future, and it is very difficult to mentor someone who is not willing to open up about what they're dealing with in their life. With that being said, I was completely candid with my spiritual mentor. I let him know everything that was going on. Nothing had manifested in the physical, but I knew that a physical response to the inappropriate thoughts I was having in my mind would be next if I did not get help.

There are times as a mentor that you may have your mentee right there next to you, right up under your wing. You may need to feed them and take care of them; but at some point, you will teach them how to fly. That's when you'll need to kick them out of the nest. Keep in mind there's an ebb and flow to the entire process. There will be times when you need to bring your mentee back close again.

Mentors have to understand that there will be times when your mentee is struggling and needs you. That is when you must be more intentional with them. At this time, my mentor brought me back in close to him. Every day for two weeks straight, we spent two to four hours together. We would pray, read the Word, and then pray some more. We spent time talking through everything.

My mentor recognized that if he didn't help me through this season, it could be detrimental to my life. Through meeting with my mentor, we realized that there were several people within our circle who were also struggling with lust. That goes back to why do life alone? It's important that we do not do life alone because there is strength in numbers. You feel stronger and more confident when you know that someone has your back.

We invited other men, my mentee included, to join us in prayer. From that, a Men's Prayer time was developed at our church. It wasn't uncommon to have fifty to seventy-five men in attendance, all praying together. That all stemmed from my mentee opening up to me as his mentor, and then me opening up to my own mentor during that process.

I went next to the second level of influence in my life, my band of brothers, my circle of friends. I was hiding my struggle with lust from them as well. None of them knew what was going on in my life. I was ashamed because of my position in the city and in the church. I was fighting my demons on my own because I wanted to save face. I didn't want anyone looking at me differently.

After sharing with my mentor, I felt more comfortable letting my band of brothers know what was going on in my life, and that's one of the best things I ever did. I was able to be transparent with them and they were transparent with me in return. Come to find out, one of my friends was dealing with lust himself. By one person opening up, it caused another person to open up, which caused another person to open up. There was a ripple effect of others getting help. This is a beautiful thing because from one person being open and honest, it set many free.

Me and my band of brothers started being more intentional with each other. We prayed for each other and sent each other scriptures. We started hanging out and fellowshipping more. This added accountability as well. At this second level, a level I like to call *the band of brothers* level, you may get a dose of medicine you don't want to hear, because you're on the same level and you respect each other the same. You may hear some strong words and more direct responses to your actions because that's who you spend more time with than anyone.

I'm so glad that I had this second level of influence in my life because it reinforced what my mentor was sharing with me. I got to hear about some of the things they were going through and some of their struggles. We began sharpening each other. Remember, iron sharpens iron. I had been keeping everything to myself, trying to sharpen my axe with wood, and all it was doing was making my axe duller.

Now, my axe was being sharpened by both my first level of influence, my mentor, as well as my second level of influence, my band of brothers. This equipped me with what I needed to affect the next level, my mentee. Everything I learned from the first two levels of influence gave me the confidence to be transparent with my mentee and let him know that I was dealing with some of the same things he was dealing with.

When I told my mentee that I had been dealing with lust, he broke down crying. He was weeping, but not because I had failed him. He was weeping because he was able to see and hear that he wasn't the only one dealing with this issue. It opened up the conversation for me and my mentee to be as real and transparent as we could. I was able to see that even though I was in his life, my mentee felt that it was impossible to live up to my level. He thought I was living a perfect life. He was relieved to know he wasn't the only one dealing with this same struggle, especially since he had built me up and never thought I would face the same battles as him. From that moment forward, I learned that I could not build myself up in my mentee's life as being a perfect person. It showed me that I needed to be more transparent with my mentees, pointing them to God and not myself.

It's dangerous for a mentor to build himself up as the hero with their mentee. The mentor is not the hero. I'll say that again because I want to make sure you get this: The mentor is not the hero. Mentors are human and make the same mistakes as others. That's why it was dangerous when my mentee was looking at me that way. There was nothing wrong with him admiring me, looking up to me, and honoring me; but I was not his hero. I was just a person walking with him down a pathway, trying to help guide him to the greatness that he was called to.

I quickly embraced my mentee and loved on him. I let him know that he was not in it alone. I was able to pay it forward and give him all the tools and wisdom that had been given to me. Not only that, but I also started bringing him along when I would hang out with my band of brothers. I brought him with me to the Men's Prayer with my spiritual mentor. I opened up my circle to him, and he was able to be around other men to glean wisdom and see that other men had his back. Now my mentee was not only benefiting from having a mentor, but he was also benefiting from his mentor's circle.

Right now, as I'm writing this book, I ask myself, "Why am I being so transparent and honest?" It's because this book is not about me. This book is about you. It's worth it to me to be open in order to give you whatever tools you need to help you maximize your life and be who you're called to be. I'm not the hero in your story. You are the hero in your story. Others are waiting for you to guide them and to be a steady voice in their life so they can fulfill the calling on their life.

Now that you've read this book, what are you going to do with the information that's been given to you? Are you going to apply some of these principles, add to the principles you already have, or are you going to continue to walk through life by yourself? I'm challenging you to apply these principles. I'm challenging you to have a mentor, to have your band of brothers, and to also have a mentee. That's how you leave a strong legacy! What type of legacy will you leave? Will you just gather everything for yourself and make it all about you? Or will you play your role, whatever that is, so you can help make this world a better place? What type of legacy will you leave?

THINK ABOUT IT.

_____

_____

_____

_____

_____

_____

_____

_____

_____

_____

_____

_____

_____

_____

_____

_____

_____

_____

_____

Author Bio

Les Thomas Sr. serves as an urban missionary providing leadership and mentoring programs to several inner-city schools. He is also the official game day host for Oklahoma State University. You'll often find him traveling as an inspirational speaker.

He is a proud husband of his lovely bride Mary for over 20 years, a loving father, and a retired Air Force veteran. He and his family are proud community members of Oklahoma City. He is passionate about building a culture of hope and giving back to his city, state, & nation.

Since a life altering encounter with his first mentor at the tender age of 12, he's been fully committed to both the process of being mentored and to paying it forward by providing mentorship and mentorship training to as many people as possible.

Made in the USA
Columbia, SC
31 August 2022

66139106R00083